TEN
THE NEW WAVE

EDITED BY

KAREN McCARTHY WOOLF

THE COMPLETE WORKS II

BLOODAXE BOOKS

Introduction copyright © Karen McCarthy Woolf 2014
Preface copyright © Nathalie Teitler 2014
Poems copyright © contributors as listed 2014

ISBN: 978 1 78037 110 8

First published 2014 by
The Complete Works,
The Albany,
Douglas Way,
London SE8 4AG
in association with
Bloodaxe Books Ltd,
Eastburn,
South Park,
Hexham,
Northumberland NE46 1BS.

www.bloodaxebooks.com
For further information about Bloodaxe titles
please visit our website or write to
the above address for a catalogue.

Cover design: Neil Astley & Pamela Robertson-Pearce.

Printed in Great Britain by Bell & Bain Limited, Glasgow, Scotland, on
acid-free paper sourced from mills with FSC chain of custody certification.

CONTENTS

10 ■ MONA ARSHI

PREFACE

'...less than 1% of poetry published by major presses in the UK is by black and Asian poets.'
Free Verse Report (2005, Arts Council England)

In 2005, Bernardine Evaristo approached Arts Council England with her concerns about the lack of publishing opportunities for poets of colour. They responded by funding the 'Free Verse' report produced by Spread the Word writer development agency, which highlighted the lack of diversity in British poetry. The actual figure of poets published in the report, as quoted above, was so shockingly low that it was clear an urgent response was required. Evaristo then initiated a national development programme for Black and Asian poets: The Complete Works (TCW), taken forward by Spread the Word.

In 2008, after an extensive national call-out, ten exceptional poets were invited to take part in the scheme In 2010, the first anthology of their work, *Ten: New Poets*, was published by Bloodaxe, edited by Evaristo and Daljit Nagra. These poets have gone on to significant success. Karen McCarthy Woolf has a collection published by Oxford/Carcanet in 2014; Roger Robinson, Seni Seneviratne and Malika Booker have published very successful collections (Peepal Tree Press) with international tours; Mir Mahfuz Ali has a first collection forthcoming from Seren; Shazea Quraishi had a pamphlet published with flipped eye and her first book-length collection is due from Bloodaxe in 2015. Most of the poets have enjoyed international residencies and publications; two (Nick Makoha and Mir Mahfuz Ali) represented their countries on the international stage of Poetry Parnassus in 2012, as did TCW II poet Kayo Chingonyi.

As project manager of the first round I felt, however, that there was still significant work to be done. Not only did the publishing figures continue to reflect low numbers but many competitions and audiences also showed the same lack of diversity. Diversity in the wider sense of its meaning to include not just a range of ethnic/cultural backgrounds but also a range of styles and approaches to poetry. In other words, the kind of genuine diversity that goes hand in hand with quality. It was for this reason that I decided it was important to take The Complete Works (TCWII) into a second round.

This second round carried on many of the distinguishing features of the first. Once again, ten exceptional poets were selected and given established and esteemed UK poets as their mentors, with Arvon residencies, bespoke seminars/salons, as well as a peer mentor or buddy from TCW I. One important difference was that the focus was now on younger poets. Almost all the poets in this anthology are under 30 and all can be considered young in poetry career terms. They demonstrate an extraordinary range of backgrounds, styles and interests. Many work cross art-forms: Inua Ellams is a successful playwright with work produced at the National Theatre, Jay Bernard is a graphic artist, Eileen Pun a highly trained martial artist.

The name of this anthology, *Ten: The New Wave*, may surprise some. After all, the last anthology was published only four years ago so it may seem premature to describe it as a new wave. I felt it was important to give it this name to highlight an important point about Black and Asian poetry in the UK; the Complete Works exists as a result of decades of hard work by BME (black minority ethnic) poets building supportive networks, communities and what can be termed a poetry *family*. In the cover letters the young poets sent in with their applications, it was astonishing how many named previous TCW poets Roger Robinson, Malika Booker, Nick Makoha and Advisory Group member, Jacob Sam-La Rose, not only as inspirations but as the reason they were writing at all. This is a new generation not only in terms of age but also because many were discovered, nurtured and informally mentored by their predecessors. This history of support, perhaps the invisible story of Black and Asian poetry in the UK, goes back further.

In 1995, Bernardine Evaristo set up the Afro-Style School at Spread the Word (of which she was then Director) delivered by Kwame Dawes (now US Patron to the Complete Works II). This was the first intensive poetry technique course run by and for poets of colour. The list of poets/writers on the course included Patience Agbabi, Chris Abani, Raman Mundair and a large number of TCW fellows. Malika's Poetry Kitchen, a writers' collective, was formed by two of these Fellows, Malika Booker and Roger Robinson, and has now been going for 15 years, offering poets a supportive space in which to develop their craft and poetics. Two of the poets on this TCW II round applied for the programme because of their desire to become part of a truly diverse community, having found little space for discussion of race/identity/different cultural approaches within mainstream British poetry. It is these initiatives, and the tireless efforts of poets working with young people (including Dorothea Smartt and Kadija George) that allows The Complete Works to flourish. The programme can in fact be seen as a way of making their hard work visible on a national and international platform.

The poets in this second anthology have already enjoyed many successes and several will go on to full collection publications by major presses next year. In 2013 Warsan Shire was named the first ever Young Poet Laureate for London and the first winner of the inaugural Brunel University African Poetry Prize. Kayo Chingonyi, like Denise Saul from TCW I before him, won the Geoffrey Dearmer Prize for Poetry. The extraordinary and exciting range of styles is beautifully explored in the introduction to this anthology.

There is little I need to add, except perhaps to answer the question Bernardine Evaristo posed in her initial anthology introduction, 'Why does it matter?' The answer to this lies in the fact that, as this collection will demonstrate, diversity and quality go hand in hand. This is the authentic diversity that comes from people expressing their own individuality with no attempt to conform. At the beginning of their journey with TCW II, the selected poets were asked to sign a contract. The first line of this contract was not, as might be expected, administrative detail, but reads; 'Be true to yourself.' It is this message that is at the heart of the programme and the anthology. And it is this truth expressed with the highest level of attention to craft and technique, which makes these poets so exceptional. There will of course be those who ask 'Yes, but why does diversity in poetry matter?' To them I would say that poetry has the potential to hold up a mirror to society; at its best, it has the ability to show what a society may become. This anthology shows us a Britain in which every voice is unique, powerful and extraordinary and every voice is heard. The importance of this, surely, does not need to be argued.

■ NATHALIE TEITLER

14

A TRUE FELLOWSHIP

As a fellow of the first round of The Complete Works, I was delighted to be asked to act as a peer-to-peer buddy for two of the new poets and to edit this anthology. Being part of what Nathalie Teitler accurately describes as The Complete Works family has been something of a poetic imperative over the past few years, both in terms of career and personal development; staying connected to the project was a way to give back and, ideally, share some of the skills one learns along the way. This collegiate approach emulates that of the far longer established US organisation Cave Canem, an African American writers' community and annual retreat founded by Toi Derricote and Cornelius Eady in 1996. Cave Canem's faculty and alumni includes many of the most prestigious – and exciting – poets writing in America today, from Major Jackson, Tyehimba Jess, Yusef Komunyakaa, Elizabeth Alexander and Terrance Hayes to the US Poet Laureate, Natasha Trethewey and Kwame Dawes, whose influence stretches to the UK where he is currently Poetry Editor at Peepal Tree Press.

Naturally, The Complete Works, with 20 fellows compared with Cave Canem's 344 is still in its infancy, although I have every faith that this community will grow and ascend. However, it would be misleading to suggest that TCW simply mimics its American prototype: the history, geographies and cultural structures of the UK and US are different and here the programme extends beyond those of African and Caribbean origin to include writers whose heritage encompasses India, Pakistan, Saudi Arabia, Sri Lanka, China and Bangladesh.

This geographic diversity is reflected in the sheer range of interest and poetics represented here, which, given that there are only ten poets, is quite remarkable. It is notable that although both Inua Ellams and Warsan Shire in particular recall a diasporic community in terms of what one might circumscribe as 'home', overall there is a commonality of rootedness in contemporary Britain that is characteristic of a more established, second or third generation experience.

Most striking, however, is the multiplicity of aesthetic influences, not just in terms of literary antecedents – which range from Thomas Sayers Ellis, Sujata Bhatt and Mirza Ghalib to Jorge Luis Borges, Du Fu and Sappho – but also with regard to medium and form: an environment proactively fostered by TCW's director Dr Nathalie Teitler, whose academic background in Latin American poetry and love of the arts in their widest sense has ensured a commitment to a climate of cross-fertilisation throughout. At the Arvon Foundation writing retreat participants were encouraged to take tango lessons, lead drawing, martial arts and meditation classes and in the seminars, and salons (which, in the spirit of the extended family unit, were opened up to applicants who made the shortlist, but not the final ten) included opportunities to collaborate and engage with musicians, visual artists and dancers. The choice of mentors, which is poet-led, also confirms this commitment, as they are equally distinct in their poetries and poetics.

In his introduction to *Identity Parade: New British & Irish Poets* (Bloodaxe Books, 2010), editor Roddy Lumsden writes of resisting the temptation to look for 'connections between the writings of those in a generation' instead identifying a culture of 'pluralism' in terms of register, subject and form. In the poetry showcased here, this pluralism is evidenced by an ambitious and adventurous engagement with language, syntax, form and approach – from Eileen Pun's exquisitely exuberant 'Some Common Whitethroat Chit-Chat' where the bird's 'Chef-hat soapy? Blondie's vanilla ice cream, Pearl's chalkin' starry' song is 'translated' into a hybrid English/nonsense/avian utterance to Jay Bernard's cacophonous 'Song of the Strike' – a choral duologue in the voice of a decapitated corpse, a poem of call and response, which in its scope and mode of address spotlights Bernard's uniquely maverick eye.

The poets who constitute this 'new wave' are for the most part, although not exclusively, under 30 – and as such occupy a different generational space to their predecessors. Nathan Hamilton, in his unapologetically feisty manifesto/opener to the anthology *Dear World & Everyone In It* (Bloodaxe Books, 2013), pinpoints a capacity for formal experiment, linguistic drama and 'ironisation' as characteristic of a new generation of young poets. Certainly, Inua Ellams' image-rich evocation of life amongst 'all the boys of Plateau Private School' owes much of its energy and driving force to his understanding of the compositional demands of theatre, and his poems within this selection are enriched by an intra-textual conceit, where he takes lines/fragments from this opening piece and expands them into subsequent yet freestanding poems. Likewise Adam Lowe's 'Vada That', which is written in Polari (a mostly gay slang) and brings an additional layer of linguistic animation to poetry that seamlessly combines queer, club and drug cultures with classical references and forms, as in 'Buzzing Affy: A Translation of Sappho's "A Hymn to Aphrodite"'.

While irony has its uses, in my view it is a strategy best employed judiciously. Too much, too often and the reader may begin to doubt the integrity of the work and its author. Thankfully, there is no doubting the intentions of the poets herein. Rishi Dastidar's witty subversions of love poems – as in 'Licking Stamps', where the muse turns her gaze on the poet to demand a billet-doux that does more than 'making sex with me/topical when it should be newsworthy' – are in their own, uncompromising way, deadly funny and in turn deadly serious; particularly in their terse and watertight construction, which is a trademark of his charismatic and singular style.

Edward Doegar, whose mentor Sean O'Brien astutely categorises him as a 'moralist, interested in what constitutes right action and in the ways in which temperament, history, luck and the permanent compromise of family life may obstruct it', achieves an elegant balance between musical intensity, philosophical quandary and lightness of touch. It is a truly assured voice that can pull off lines as simple as 'I step from the porch into rain/A blessing//Today even the gutter-water/Will be fresh' (from 'April – After Li Po'). Lightness of touch is an attribute Doegar shares with Mona Arshi, whose poems of family life and loss take on the weight of bereavement, in this case the death of a sibling, with a delicacy that belies their force. 'Notes Towards an Elegy' is a poem that exemplifies her ability to transform trauma into a poetry that is simultaneously urgent and complex in its imaginative and conceptual movement.

Last summer I spent some time thinking about the lyric essay and how the tensions between the intellect and a more visceral sensibility might combine. Then Sarah Howe's sequence 'from *A Certain Chinese Encyclopedia*' (extracted here in part) landed on my desk. Howe is a scholar and an academic, and thus the fusion of the lyric voice with a tougher, cerebral and intertextual structure that requires its reader to think and to think hard, appears quite effortless in its execution. The poems also explore Howe's Chinese and mixed-race heritage – not in a direct, autobiographical manner, but through a literary and cultural historicism, most explicitly perhaps in 'Others' where the dynamics of identity politics and race, itself 'a terrible pun', are critiqued through a multi-lingual process of etymological enquiry. Kayo Chingonyi also scrutinises identity in his sequence '*calling a spade a spade*', and as the title suggests, the nuances of language and its impact on the individual and collective psyche is a fruitful preoccupation. Written as a series of tightly controlled, 11-line monologues in the voice of a world-weary thespian, a black actor who having spent most of his life battling the indignities of typecasting knows how to 'stifle a laugh/at the playwright's misplaced *get me, blud* and *safe*', these are poems that refuse to let anyone off the hook. Here 'The N Word' might be found 'Lounging in a Pinter script/or pitched from a Transit van's rolled-down window' – a phrase that cannot fail to remind the reader that even in these heady days of multicultural homogeneity, the subtleties and brutality of racism are proximate and intertwined.

Warsan Shire is the poet who opens this anthology, which is arranged in reverse alphabetical order. Of all the writers gathered here Shire is the most cinematic, in terms of both influence and effect. The events in her specular poem 'Backwards' play out like a speeded-up version of Christopher Nolan's 'Memento'. Then there is 'Men in Cars', a collection of Altman-esque vignettes where a woman remembers having sex with men via the make of car: in the BMW she catches her own reflection in the rearview mirror, her head 'bobbing like a saint on the dashboard'. It is this cool, unflinching eye for detail that renders Shire's work so magnetic. Yet there is also an immense compassion: for her community as a young Somali and for the women and family members whose stories she narrates so eloquently.

So, amongst all this difference, what binds these multi-cultural poets together? If anything, I might suggest a certain confidence: a confidence to pursue idiosyncratic avenues; to embrace, ignore or transcend the political; to write from or for a community if they so choose; to cast the net of cultural and literary influence wide and to be writers who realise that sophistication springs from the complex and the simple, from subversion and sincerity. At a time when the economic pressures on poetry publishing – and book publishing in general for that matter – are profound, the opportunity to be heard is all the more hard won. These are voices that demand to be considered on their own terms – a 'luxury' for which earlier generations have helped to pave the way.

In her Preface to this volume Nathalie Teitler refers to the contract the poets signed: at the heart of The Complete Works is a bid to nurture diversity in all its forms, and thus while the maxim 'be true to yourself' could never quite be called a 'manifesto' (a declaration which in itself surely provokes uniformity?) it could be described as a motto and one which these poets have demonstrably taken to heart.

■ KAREN McCARTHY WOOLF

WARSAN SHIRE

■ **WARSAN SHIRE** was born in Kenya to Somali parents and is the Young Poet Laureate for London. She is the poetry editor at *SPOOK* magazine and her national and international readings include the Aldeburgh Poetry Festival, Badalisha Poetry Festival in Cape Town, StoryMoja Hay Festival and Kwani Literature Festival in Nairobi, Ferrara Poetry Festival in Italy, House of Culture in Berlin, Festival of Utopia in Copenhagen, alongside various venues in Canada, the US and UK such as the Royal Festival Hall, British Museum and Serpentine Gallery. Her début work *Teaching My Mother How to Give Birth* (flipped eye) was published in 2011. Warsan curates workshops around healing, trauma and poetry therapy. Her poems are published in *Wasafiri, Magma, Poetry Review* and *The Salt Book of Younger Poets* (Salt, 2011). She was the winner of the inaugural Brunel University African Poetry Prize. ■

■ PASCALE PETIT:

Warsan Shire was born in Kenya, is Somali and has lived in London most of her life. She draws on her rich heritage, and a wealth of stories told to her by her family, to write extraordinary poems of broad appeal and intimate address. But these documents from the hybrid zone of London–Mogadishu are far from prose. There's a musicality to her cadences, as in 'The Ugly Daughter', where the resonant last line 'but God, / doesn't she wear / the world well?' gains its memorability not just through the vivid metaphor of a girl wearing the earth but also through the sonic chime of wear/world/well.

What is particularly distinctive about her work is how it cuts through literary contrivance and the distancing devices of much of British poetry, and this urgency, coupled with lyrical facility, has already earned her accolades. Although still in her twenties, Warsan won the inaugural 2013 Brunel University African Poetry Prize and is appointed first Young Poet Laureate of London.

She brings intense reports of diaspora experience to her writing, especially about women's concerns, but her themes are universal: love, sex, war, trauma, loneliness and identity. While her topics can be shocking, what is striking is the warmth and disarming candour with which she transforms her material. 'The House' uses the extended metaphor of a woman as a home. The trope is not new, but the speaking voice has a confiding tone despite its wide reach: 'At parties I point to my body and say *This is where love comes to die. Welcome, come in, make yourself at home*'.

As well as a flair for intense imagery, Warsan has a gift for creating aphoristic two-liners: 'Mother says there are locked rooms inside all women,/kitchen of lust, bedroom of grief, bathroom of apathy.' (The House) Even when embedded in longer lyrics, it's easy to pick out stand-alone lines, lines that translate seamlessly to the soundbite and as such are suited to technology platforms such as Twitter, where she has a devoted following, perhaps also because she boldly broaches taboo areas most poets shy away from.

An example of this courage is in 'Sara', which presents the custom of female genital mutilation from an informed viewpoint. Unusually, we are given an insight into the practice and its effect on young lives from a boy's perspective, through a devastating image: '*Imagine*, he says, pointing to my mouth,/ *pushing an entire finger* / / *into the gap* / *between your front teeth*'.

This ability to speak from multiple viewpoints reveals versatility. Her cast of characters, especially women, are sympathetic in their humanness, and above all in their bid to reclaim power. This bid is at the heart of Warsan's art. ■

Backwards

(for Saaid Shire)

The poem can start with him walking backwards into a room.
He takes off his jacket and sits down for the rest of his life,
that's how we bring Dad back.
I can make the blood run back up my nose, ants rushing into a hole.
We grow into smaller bodies, my breasts disappear,
your cheeks soften, teeth sink back into gums.
I can make us loved, just say the word.
Give them stumps for hands if even once they touched us without
                consent,
I can write the poem and make it disappear.
Step Dad spits liquor back into glass,
Mum's body rolls back up the stairs, the bone pops back into place,
maybe she keeps the baby.
Maybe we're okay kid?
I'll rewrite this whole life and this time there'll be so much love,
you won't be able to see beyond it.

You won't be able to see beyond it,
I'll rewrite this whole life and this time there'll be so much love.
Maybe we're okay kid,
maybe she keeps the baby.
Mum's body rolls back up the stairs, the bone pops back into place,
Step Dad spits liquor back into glass.
I can write the poem and make it disappear,
give them stumps for hands if even once they touched us without
                consent,
I can make us loved, just say the word.
Your cheeks soften, teeth sink back into gums
we grow into smaller bodies, my breasts disappear.

25

I can make the blood run back up my nose, ants rushing into a hole,
that's how we bring Dad back.
He takes off his jacket and sits down for the rest of his life.
The poem can start with him walking backwards into a room.

Men in Cars

Nissan

In the back of that car that night when I thought even God had turned his back on me, I felt your hands around my neck and I bit your shoulder until you fizzed, I told you to *Get off*. You said *No*, and I said *No*, how many times? I can't remember.

BMW

In the back of the car one evening, my first kiss with a man too old, I'm 15 years old and he's a boxer who failed his last piss test, the car is very hot but I refuse to take off my jacket. It's London and it's November and I close my eyes and I say *Just do it* and he does, I catch my own reflection in the rearview mirror, my head bobbing like a saint on a dashboard.

Honda

In the back of his mother's car I whisper *It's not going to happen for me, just go ahead* and he spits on his fingers but still nothing happens. He has silver coins for eyes, the windows are too misty to see through. After, I touch the back of his head with my young hands to comfort his failed magic trick, the gold ring on my finger stares back at me.

Volvo

In the back of my mind I hold all their names and the licence plate numbers of their cars. This last one had sweaty hands and rubbed the excess on my leg. The car was filled with weed smoke, I would emerge from it like a contestant on a singing show. He said that he'd dreamt all my hair had turned white and I wore a long white dress. I asked *What do you think that means?* He smiled, his silver tooth blinking under the streetlamp that lit up the driver's side and said *Fuck if I know.*

Sara

I

We typed the word *clitoris* in to Google
and found a numbered diagram,
then spent hours with a small mirror,
comparing.

II

That one night when Sara
got into a car with a boy,
we all knew it was a mistake.
No one said anything when she

walked back smiling, limping.
We sat there ruined,
watching her spit-clean blood
from the mouth of her skirt.

III

In the lunchroom, Hussein tells us
what it felt like for him. We're mesmerised.
Imagine, he says, pointing to my mouth,
pushing an entire finger

into the gap
between your front teeth.
The girl beside me shudders,
I touch the chalk of my teeth with my tongue.

You know she begged me? Even though it
hurt she still begged me, kept whispering:
make me normal, please
make me normal, open me up.

Midnight in the Foreign Food Aisle

Dear Uncle, is everything you love foreign
or are you foreign to everything you love?
We're all animals and the body wants what it wants,
I know. The blonde said *Come in, take off*
your coat and what do you want to drink?
Love is not haram but after years of fucking
women who cannot pronounce your name,
you find yourself in the foreign food aisle,
pressing your face into the ground, praying
in a language you haven't used in years.

Haram

My older sister soaps between her legs, her hair

a prayer of curls. When she was my age, she stole
the neighbour's husband, burnt his name into her skin.
For weeks she smelt of cheap perfume and dying flesh.

It's 4am and she winks at me, bending over the sink,
her small breasts bruised from sucking.
She smiles, pops her gum before saying
boys are haram, don't ever forget that.

Some nights I hear her in her room screaming.
We play Surah Al-Baqarah to drown her out.
Anything that leaves her mouth sounds like sex.
Our mother has banned her from saying God's name.

The Ugly Daughter

knows loss intimately,
carries whole cities in her belly.

As a child, relatives wouldn't hold her.
She was splintered wood and seawater.
They said she reminded them of the war.

On her fifteenth birthday you taught her
how to tie her hair like rope
and smoke it over burning frankincense.

You made her gargle rosewater
and while she coughed, said
*Macaanto girls shouldn't smell
of lonely or empty.*

You're her mother.
Why did you not warn her?
Hold her, tell her that men will not love her
if she is covered in continents,
if her teeth are small colonies,
if her stomach is an island,
if her thighs are borders?

What man wants to lie down
and watch the world burn
in his bedroom?

Your daughter's face is a small riot,
her hands are a civil war,
a refugee camp behind each ear,
a body littered with ugly things

but God,
doesn't she wear
the world well.

The House

I

Mother says there are locked rooms inside all women,
kitchen of lust, bedroom of grief, bathroom of apathy.
Sometimes the men they come with keys,
and sometimes the men they come with hammers.

II

Nin soo joog laga waayo, soo jiifso aa laga helaa,
I said Stop, I said No and he did not listen.

III

Perhaps Rihanna has a plan, perhaps she takes Chris back to hers
only for him to wake up hours later in a bathtub full of ice,
with a dry mouth, looking down at his new, neat procedure.

IV

I point to my body and say *Oh this old thing? No, I just slipped
    it on.*

V

Are you going to eat that? I say to my mother, pointing to my
father who is lying on the dining-room table, his mouth stuffed
with a red apple.

VI

The bigger my body is, the more locked rooms there are, the more men come with keys. Adam didn't push it all the way in, I still think about what he could have opened up inside of me. Bashin came and hesitated at the door for three years. Johnny with the blue eyes came with a bag of tools he had used on other women: one hairpin, a bottle of bleach, a switchblade and a jar of Vaseline. Yonis called out God's name through the keyhole and no one answered. Some begged, some climbed the side of my body looking for a window, some said they were on their way and did not come.

VII

Show us on the doll where you were touched, they said.
I said I don't look like a doll, I look like a house.
They said Show us on the house.

Like this: two fingers in the jam jar
Like this: an elbow in the bathwater
Like this: a hand in the drawer.

VIII

I should tell you about my first love who found a trapdoor under my left breast nine years ago, fell in and hasn't been seen since. Every now and then I feel something crawling up my thigh. He should make himself known, I'd probably let him out. I hope he hasn't bumped in to the others, the missing boys from small towns, with pleasant mothers, who did bad things and got lost in the maze of my hair. I treat them well enough, a slice of bread, if they're lucky a piece of fruit. Except for Johnny with the blue eyes, who picked

my locks and crawled in. Silly boy, chained to the basement
of my fears, I play music to drown him out.

IX

Knock knock.
Who's there?
No one.

X

At parties I point to my body and say *This is where love comes
to die. Welcome, come in, make yourself at home.* Everyone laughs,
they think I'm joking.

EILEEN PUN

■ **EILEEN PUN** was born in New York and is the daughter of Haitian and Haitian-Chinese parents. She is widely travelled and has lived and worked in the United States, Italy and China. Since she emigrated to Britain she has lived in various parts of the North West and currently lives in Grasmere in the Lake District. In 2011 Eileen was selected as an Escalator poetry prizewinner by Writers' Centre Norwich and also awarded a writing and research grant by Arts Council England. ■

Eileen Pun's poetry is complex, careful and shot through with a strong sense of the conditionality of language and identity. Nothing is taken for granted in her writing, every word is hard-won and decided. When I began reading her poems I had the sense of a sculptor, someone who has to invest physical effort into the placing of each word on the page and the chiselling out of each line, someone for whom the word is a real and living being, drawing along webs and tissues of meanings and constantly inflecting itself in the light of each new insight. A poet who understands that poems derive from the craft-like act of selecting and interweaving words, and that words themselves are full of multiplicity and duplicity.

In a similar way the narratives of her poems are conditional and eccentric. She chooses situations which are unheroic, almost documentary: the hanging out of washing, a snapshot of life in a studio flat, and she probes each of these scenes from the most oblique angles, revealing views which remind me of the peepshow boxes of the Flemish painters: we are hidden viewers of scenes apparently laid out to indicate proportion, but which function with a grammar of proportion which is profoundly unsettling.

Her poems are full of competing, conflicting voices: the third-person narrative often slips into a first-person inter-jection, an overheard conversation, a piece of 'found' text or a quote or song. Sometimes the voices contradict each other sharply, or muse on the apparent truth of the narrative as a whole. The effect is destabilising: the reader rapidly learns to question and mistrust the authority of the poem.

This oblique view must come at least partly from Eileen Pun's circumstances. She is the child of Haitian and Haitian-Chinese immigrants, she was born in New York and grew up in Florida, but without any sense of allegiance to her Floridian surroundings. She left the USA as a student and never returned. She writes of her linguistic background: '"*Where* is your accent from?" is a difficult question. As the daughter of two immigrant Haitian and Haitian-Chinese parents, I thoroughly understand that my "language" has not been realised without language trade-offs, and loss, and also sacrifice.'

Eileen studied international politics, rather than literature, which she says has given her the sense of being a 'gate-crashing poet', a poet who hasn't studied the craft, or inherited the poetic mantle. In fact this reluctance to appropriate the genre, or to assume mastery is at one with her poetic project: she comes to poetry as a constant stranger, and it is that sense of precise estrangement that makes her work so distinctive. Recently she has written versions of a poem by the Chinese poet Du Fu. The poem is a reflection on a dancer the poet once saw perform, and in Eileen's version the remembered joy at the dancer's beauty is counterpointed with the distinctly modern exclamations of another speaker. Perception and the resulting artistic creation are the subjects of Eileen's version, she stands at one remove from the original poem and translates its dynamics rather than its words, analysing the effect of art as she writes it.

All this might suggest a personal detachment or 'rootlessness', which in fact couldn't be further from the truth. Eileen lives in Grasmere, where I visited her for a walk up onto Helm Crag, talking poetry until we were stunned into silence by the view on that late afternoon. Eileen's love of landscape and the details of her surroundings are palpable in her conversation as well as her poetry. Her poems about birds demonstrate her absolute faith in small detail and close observation. The birds, like her, are both migratory and rooted:

she writes of the Lesser Whitethroat,

> You are an orphan
> but you also have many kin.

Chi mangia e non invita, possa strozzarsi con ogni mollica.
He who eats alone and invites no one, will choke with every crumb.
— ITALIAN SAYING

Mollica: Southern Italian meaning 'crumb', 'soft part (of bread)',
nickname for a soft-hearted one.

Truffle Hunter

Well, this truffle hunter will choke on every crumb.

What woman could stand the cold hell of his unkempt,
stone house? Hear him whistle, hour-in, hour-out
that irksome jingle to arouse the dogs. *Fi-fa! Chu-cho!*
Lu-lu!

Singing their names as he straps their muzzles on.

Off like a hero, into mid-afternoon or into sunrise
too, or into deepest, greenest night. Don't trap him
to times or sayings, irrelevant as wives. Leave him
to his cigarette and unchecked habits – impenetrable
and on guard –

eating with one arm, cradling a plate with the other.

Any casual he takes on
must not go beyond,
                                    never touch the dogs,

nor linger after work because,
someone has to mind the warm and rising

bread, when bread was never asked for. Better not

live in a house riddled with *mollicas*. Tell him *who?*
Who is meant to tidy up then? Not a casual and not *him* –
too busy swearing on the weather, or the Madonna
when church bells are ringing a wedding. He knows

no woman could take the burs – never-ending
like the faults that stick to him, dragged into
their complication – contempt hiding in the linen.
Their spikes will only put marks against him.

Beside herself in a double bed

                        she would have to pluck them off,

connect hour to odd, dry, hour

                    unable to be rid of them. How could he

hide his joy? The night he takes Lulu – *sharp bitch
that she is* – into the woods and she detects a longing.
Its timbre is a red so explicit her ears stand pricked.

Now the sky promises snow, a weather to urge them.

                    She takes him
to a young oak. So many promises. He is whispering
everything he is willing to owe. This truffle hunter
doesn't feel the alter in his surroundings. This air

                    markedly colder as he falls
to his knees, pushes up his sleeves, shoves Lulu's eager
face out of his way and digs through the darkness alone
                        – lost
until the light changes, the phantom hooks, the sky breaks.

Gaily he carries *that jingle* on his lips. He must get back
to the house that will be frozen blue-violet with waiting.
Already he is thinking of that soft, patient, bread. How he will
tuck in, hands covered in dirt and the aphrodisiac of pigs.

For Carlo, My Neighbour

PART I

I am thinking about Carlo and the very first time we met.
He put his washing out, like a range of conditions:
underpants to woolly cardigans, all undergoing refreshment.
He left spaces, yes, but they were odd and unserviceable.
So this line is all for Carlo, the not so young Carlo, *so what?*
He is of today's August character, naturally an inexact man,
a plural colour, like peach, a chalky voice, an erasable edge.
His house with the door wide open is shelter to unappreciated operas.
That morning, yapping to him as he weighted the line, 'La Traviata'.
The Chatham Court neighbourhood communal, also called 'the
        common'
should be more social, but in practice we choose to dry out alone.
I lift my head like you might pull out a bookmark, or raise a toast.

PART II

I go across with my arms full of wet washing – to stand
face-to-face with the mighty geometry that is another's.
I'm full of gusto, open with, 'I have nowhere. Nowhere.'
He goes, 'Let me make you a coffee.' which sounds like, 'Bravo!'
'Now?' I say, and a whole day squeaks out from the slack in my bicep,
the very day that I begin to separate what could and could not wait.
And he says, 'Maybe one day I can even make a macaroni for you.'
to which I start laughing. A coltish wind, through the clothesline
like voodoo. Shapes of bodies possessed then left, giddy
with stress only to be bucked by relaxation, indeterminate
knowing and un-knowing. Funny, funny macaroni.

45

Goodly Gongsun

(after Du Fu's 'A Song of Dagger Dancing to a Girl Pupil of Lady Gongsun')

I *Painter*

> *I watched Lady Gongsun perform a sword dance, like a floating boat in deep water hit by the swift patter of rain. I knew all the top performers of the Pear Garden troupe, and I knew the best performers outside the troupe – there was none as Lady Gongsun.*

Goodness, sure. I will always remember the dancer. Light-
        heartedly,
I conjure her. I pirouette my brush and begin sketching – peak
followed by its mountain, woodland, the wild birds that surely live
in them. Then I listen until their calls turned echoes have drawn
me in, good heavens. Good heavens, I sigh while shaking my head.
I could take off decades like that, moving back and forth and back.
So wantonly age falls away, not one but nine suns at a time.
Good riddance to it all, especially the heavy blue. Even the birds
that I have drawn have taken off using their own dragon-wings.
There was nothing before her dance began, nothing at all –
then suddenly her unibrow in a furrow. Have mercy!
Good Lord, there is no rest between her thighs.

II *Calligrapher*

> *Even the great calligrapher from Wu named Zhang Zu –*
> *famous for his wild running hand – beheld Lady Gongsun*
> *performing the Western River Sword Dance. He watched*
> *her whenever she danced in Ye County, making great*
> *strides in his cursive calligraphy.*

Bride sheet
blanch rice grain
dark thoughts
light strokes
the stains

Some Common Whitethroat Chit-Chat

(or, a couple of common whitethroats having a crack)

Albino!
Albino!

Q-tip! Albino!   School glue?
Teethy Dove-y… teethy.   School glue?

Marshmallow. Goos-ey, cotton-y marshmallow.
Golfballs! Maaarsshmaalloow?   Icing Blondie? Platinum Blondie?

Chalk Blondie.   *Pearl.*
Pearl?!   Sugar crystallin'-'fleur-de-lis'-cloudy-cloudy Pearl?

Snow?!   *Pearl…* Ivory, radish flesh, tartare sauce, Pearl.
Painter's trousers Dove-y.   Cricket trousers!   Dove-y?!

Chef-hat Q-tip. Dove-y avalanches Pearl's coconut meat. Blanc?
PEARL FRENCH MANICURED STARS!

Milky swan!
Milky?! Milky?! Fondant surfing Pearl…   Sea-gulling Blondie…

Blondie's snowdropped. Blondie's correction fluid.
Salty Dove-y.   Blondie's *wedding dress?* Blondie's *aspirin?*

Chef-hat soapy? Blondie's vanilla ice cream, Pearl's chalkin' starry!
Lima beans.

Knuckle-grip Q-tip.
Turtle-Dove-y…   Pearl's lima beans.

48

Knu-ckle-grip 'Pearl's lima beans'.
Seafoam blizzards smoke, smoke blizzards boiled albumen.

KNU-CKLE GRIP 'PEARL'S LIMA BEANS!'
Piiic – keeeet – fencccce cumulo-nimbus sour cream.
          BEARD OF GOD!

Scratch concrete beer head. FLAG OF SURRENDER?!
Flag of surrender!   *Beard of God…*

Beard of Santa Claus baby powder.   Pearl's Dovey's. *Blanc?*
Blanc… teethy… Pearl's snowballin',   Pearl's snowballin'.

Lesser Whitethroat

Something disappears.

Pressed grass where weight should have been,
              a tree limb uncontrollably shaking,
         leaves on their way down,
              the mind rattling under a hat-brim
    a cat, blank off the ground –
                   nightfall.

Make this the opening that you prayed for.

              You can change sides,
    scale the wall, distill every one of your wishes
       into the bandit's bliss.   Lift yourself,

         and you will flow through a thousand airs –
    with each adjustment you might lose strength,
nevertheless,
         climb and take height
    climb and take one story at a time.

    Land light above a window, a busy kitchen
         is best,
       the room with the burning hearth will also do.
    Take in the fragrance of daily life,
but do not take part.   Your feet might walk rooftops,
              but your head graces heaven –
shoulder to shoulder with the incense and graspless.

Wherever you find doorways, slip in as if indigenous –
        or a hole –
    keep your breathing pressed,
less, lesser, less...
        Yes!
                You are the size of a mouse
the introverted house guest,
    whether you are dressed in monk's grey,
    the dusty cloak of an old mountain hag...

    if you are seen
    to be a man, not a man –
                your feathers remain the same.
If anyone should ask, your Western name
                        is Sylvia.
    Do you understand?
Remember, if you are caught, you are neither
                        our son nor our daughter.
    You are an orphan,
    but you also have many kin –
        in the Sahara, Arabia, India, Mongolia...
            even Siberia, such ideas are comforting.

Remember everything you have accomplished
    everybody you love... then drop them over the edge.
        Now you are lesser,
                    more enlightened,
        Yes?
    If you should be mistaken for a common
    thief, if you are about to lose your hand –
                make your heart stay red,
seal your mouth and freeze your throat.

51

At your centre you shall hurt
until you glow.

I am afraid
you will find there is nowhere else to go.
There are so many thorns in the hedgerow – the land fruitless.

The mountain pass?   *Impossible*
under this new snow.

Studio Apartment: Sunday

Sunset honeys the bijou palace. Its dweller wishes
to turn the soft, grey page of a newspaper until his leisure
becomes unbearable. He senses nothing of merit can ever
happen in here. Neither a succession of great decisions,
nor great love.

It seems the studio and its dweller will fill and
empty like any good organ. Gold flecks on the glass
of wine that he is drinking from, the mandolin lies aslant
on the rented sofa (although, only an hour ago, it was seeking
so much playfulness).

He begins peeling a clementine. Now, this is very much
like the introductory part of an evening spent kissing – citrusy.
The bijou flares of gold bead oil miasma, while its dweller
derives and derives – thumbing the natural breaks
of what will come off, next.

ADAM LOWE

■ **ADAM LOWE** is a writer, publisher and creative producer from Leeds who now lives in Manchester. In 2013, he was LGBT History Month Poet Laureate and is leading the Manchester Pride Writers in Residence programme. He was nominated for the Venture Award and runs Young Enigma, a Manchester-based writing and performance collective which supports emerging artists who self-identify as LGBT or queer. Adam was selected as Yorkshire's poet for the Olympics, as part of the National Lottery's 12 Poets of 2012 competition. He was a Youth Ambassador for the Cultural Olympiad. His 2012 collection *Precocious* (Dog Horn Publishing, 2012) was a reader nomination for the *Guardian* First Book Award. He is of Caribbean-Irish-English heritage. ■

■ PATIENCE AGBABI:

Adam Lowe is a multi-faceted writer: poet, novelist, playwright, producer, his work is rooted in the gay community where he regularly supports the professional development of other young writers. He draws his principal inspiration from Manchester's dynamic gay scene and is particularly attracted to 'high camp', which has resulted in creatively innovative performance art collaborations, for example he was producer for Young Enigma's 'A Royal Wedding' at Manchester Pride 2013. His poetry often recasts the figure of the queen or the goddess into the 21st century.

What impresses me most about Adam's work is his ability to merge the subversive contemporary with the classics. He is equally at home with Greek mythology, fairy tales and the Bible as with queer club culture. This is rare on the poetry scene and renders his work cutting edge and multi-layered. There is often a strong emphasis on the physicality of the body. In 'Afterlife @ Aftershock', we are invited to descend into a postmodern underworld with a 'three-headed bouncer' and a DJ, 'hand cutting tunes like/a scythe'. This classical remix skilfully captures the drug-induced disorientation of underground club culture.

This classical-contemporary sensibility also shows in Adam's unaccented formal verse. His poems are often in regular stanza lengths with occasional internal rhyme to enhance musicality. He is attracted to the dramatic tension of the couplet or the tightness of the sonnet. He has also translated Sappho's 'A Hymn to Aphrodite' into snappy colloquialisms, yet retaining the technically-challenging Sapphic stanza. A regular performer of his work, Adam appreciates how the music of a poem is integral to its meaning. His most exciting work to date uses the theatrical gay slang, Polari, to which he has added his own neologisms. 'Vada That', reined into tercets, 'blows//lamors through the oxy at all/the passing trade.' This is language both playful and challenging, buzzing with potential. I look forward to seeing how Adam develops his poetic style in the future. ■

The Kiss

We kiss in front of your monument,
our lips pressed like this, the ovals
of mouths bunched into fists.

We hold tight with soft arms,
and tango in rows, our bodies
all faces and hooked elbows.

We kiss outside parliament
to show you we're here. We kiss
in the street. We kiss without fear.

Tryst with the Devil

Come. Let me show you dewy wonders
here in the grass. Let me feel the flicker
of your tongue in my arse. Come

slide over me, muscular river,
rockstar-pornstar in the shape of an asp.
Splash your coat of stars across me.

Wrap me in your night. Prophet
of rebels, let me taste your dissent;
wet me with your meteorites; with tongue

I'll trace your proud descent. King of things
that scrabble in the dirt, raise
your fallen army – drive it through me.

Afterlife @ Aftershock

Pass the dry-ice strobe-stare of the
three-headed bouncer there, pass
the hellhound with six black shoulders.
Descend with me into a bruise-lit underworld.
Anna Phylactic, our Queen Ishtar, rules
with eye-patch, hoop-skirt, wig.
Cyclopean giver of asphodel foams
at his grinning mouth, collects payment from
all to lift them, high spirits, to heaven;
and the DJ, hand cutting tunes like
a scythe, ferries us to the shore of the next
blue dawn. Bass rumbles, the displeasure
of life against ecstasy; then the drop comes
and we're wing-swept to rapture as one.

Vada That

Aunt nell the patter flash and gardy loo!
Bijou, she trolls, bold, on lallies
slick as stripes down the Dilly.

She minces past the brandy latch
to vada dolly dish for trade, silly
with oomph and taste to park.

She'll reef you on her vagaries –
should you be so lucky. She plans
to gam a steamer and tip the brandy,

but give her starters and she'll be happy
to give up for the harva. Mais oui,
she's got your number, duckie.

She'll cruise an omi with fabulosa bod,
regard the scotches, the thews, the rod –
charpering a carsey for the trick.

Slick, she bamboozles the ogles
of old Lilly Law. She swishes
through town, 'alf meshigener, and blows

lamors through the oxy at all
the passing trade. She'll sass a drink
of aqua da vida, wallop with vera in claw.

Nellyarda her voche's chant till the nochy
with panache becomes journo, till
the sparkle laus the munge out of guard.

But sharda she's got nada, she aches
for an affaire, and dreams of pogey
through years of nix. The game nanti works

– not for her. She prefers a head
or back slum to the meat rack. Fact is,
she'll end up in the charpering carsey

of Jennifer Justice. What is this
queer ken she's in? Give her an auntie
or a mama. The bones isn't needed just yet.

Though she's a bimbo bit of hard,
she's royal and tart. And girl, you know
vadaing her eek is always bona.

Affaire: a lover, a serious partner. *Auntie*: older gay man, role model.
Aunt nell: ear, listen (also: *nellyarda*). *Back slum*: public lavatory.
Bona: good. *The bones*: a boyfriend or husband. *Brandy*: bottom
(from Cockney rhyming slang: 'brandy and rum'). *Charpering*:
finding. *Charpering carsey*: police cell. *The Dilly*: Piccadilly, a high
street or similar. *Dolly*: pretty. *Eek*: face. *Gardy loo*: 'Look out!'
Harva: anal sex. *Head*: bed. *Journo*: day. *Lallies*: legs. *Laus*: chases.
Mama: mentor. *Meat rack*: brothel. *Munge*: darkness. *Nochy*: night.
Omi: man. *Patter flash*: gossip, chat. *Pogey*: money. *Reef*: to feel,
to grope (especially the bulge or crotch). *Sharda*: though. *Scotches*:
legs. *Thews*: thighs, sinews. *Troll*: walk. *Vada*: see, spy, look. *Vera*:
gin (from Cockney rhyming slang: 'Vera Lynn').

Buzzing Affy

A translation of Sappho's 'A Hymn to Aphrodite'

I

Sister, on your precious throne of metal bling,
funking daughter of jagged skies and lightning,
domme* of odes, listen close now, come on. Sister,
       I'm woman calling.

Listen how you listen, catch my morning buzz,
my voice carried over wire and horizon,
just come, as you came before. Sister, leave your
       strobe-light happening.

II

Your arrival is the tide-ripple of doves,
ecstasy's muscle-rhythm through the club.
You lift high over skies, glow stick bright, throw down
       heavens to hip-wind.

The haters still come. And you – my avatar,
cover girl, superstar – wait while I sulk! Quick,
blow kisses when you text back. Spit me a rap, girl,
       I need your reply.

III

You will say: *Who has dissed you this time, sister?*
Who stole your dark-kissed heart? Can you take it back?
They'll soon give all that you gave, then give you more.
       They always return.

63

Tell me who to petition, who to burn out,
who to placard – you promised me this, sister.
Come now. Keep your vow. This world could soon be ours.
Be my damn lover.

* Domme: a dominant female in a BDSM relationship.

Tough Look

Well then, that's how you'll move:
with purpose; leonine strides.

You'll thatch your skin thicker
with a patchwork of diva, all Liza,

Whitney, Marilyn. You'll scare
men who fall out of Wetherspoons,

invoke platitudes from girls streaked
the colour of shoe polish. You'll

be you: a little braver, a little bigger
– but it will always sting inside.

SARAH HOWE

■ **SARAH HOWE** was born in Hong Kong, to an English father and Chinese mother, before moving to the UK as a child. She studied at Cambridge and later as a Kennedy Scholar at Harvard. She is currently a Research Fellow at Gonville and Caius College, Cambridge, where she teaches English literature. Her debut pamphlet of poems, *A Certain Chinese Encyclopedia* (Tall-Lighthouse) won an Eric Gregory Award from the Society of Authors in 2010. Her first book of poems is forthcoming from Chatto & Windus in 2015. ■

■ W.N. HERBERT:

I first encountered Sarah Howe's work while judging the Arts Foundation poetry award, and was highly impressed by the combination of lyrical deftness and intellectual clarity in her work. So I jumped at the chance to work with her on this project. She has the serious poet's unerring knack for finding the clearest possible subject matter that will at once illustrate the underlying themes and concerns of her work; and demonstrate her originality of thought – an action which, precisely notated, becomes 'style'. This is evidenced by the poems here from the sequence 'A Certain Chinese Encyclopedia'.

This takes its thematic and structural principle from an essay by Borges in which he refers to a taxonomy of animals which, he alleges, is Chinese. Its fourteen elements supply her with the subjects for fourteen poems – everything from 'sucking pigs' to creatures 'that from a long way off look like flies'.

The idea of an over-arching rationale or meta-structure is important here, and is indeed characteristic of her way of working. Fourteen is, of course, the number of lines in a sonnet, and together the fourteen poems interact with each other in a way that recalls the formal dynamics operating between the different parts of the sonnet.

The combination of cogent analysis and apparent eccentricity in these elements offer a precise analogy for two of the main concerns in this work: the relationship between the academic and the poetic – often assumed to result in an 'experimental' mode of writing; and the tensions between Chinese and Western aspects of her identity. Instead of dividing these themes into separate subject areas or ways of working, she seeks to encompass them within a single field of poetic tensions in much the same way they operate within her ordinary life as complementary aspects of professional and personal identity. ■

from A Certain Chinese Encyclopedia

> *These ambiguities, redundancies, and deficiencies recall those attributed by Dr Franz Kuhn to a certain Chinese encyclopedia entitled* The Celestial Emporium of Benevolent Knowledge. *On those remote pages it is written that animals are divided into: (a) belonging to the Emperor, (b) embalmed, (c) tame, (d) sucking pigs, (e) sirens, (f) fabulous, (g) stray dogs, (h) included in the present classification, (i) frenzied, (j) innumerable, (k) drawn with a very fine camelhair brush, (l) others, (m) having just broken the water pitcher, (n) that from a long way off look like flies.*

> JORGE LUIS BORGES

Tame

> *It is more profitable to raise geese than daughters.*
> CHINESE PROVERB

This is the tale of the woodsman's daughter. Born with a box
     of ashes set beside the bed,
in case. Before the baby cried, he rolled her face into the cinders –
     held it. Weak from the bloom
of too-much-blood, the new mother tried to stop his hand. He
                         dragged
     her out into the yard, flogged her
with the usual branch. If it was magic in the wood, they never
     said, but she began to change:

her scar-ridged back, beneath his lashes, toughened to a rind; it split
   and crusted into bark. Her prone
knees dug in the sandy ground and rooted, questing for water,
   as her work-grained fingers lengthened
into twigs. The tree – a lychee – he continued to curse as if it
   were his wife – its useless, meagre
fruit. Meanwhile the girl survived. Feathered in a fluff of greyish ash,
   her face tucked in, a little gosling.

He called her Mei Ming: *No Name.* She never learned to speak.
                                                        Her life
   was maimed by her father's sorrow.
For grief is a powerful thing – even for objects never conceived.
   He should have dropped her down
the well. Then at least he could forget. Sometimes when he set
   to work, hefting up his axe
to watch the cleanness of its arc, she butted at his elbow – again,
   again – with her restive head,

till angry, he flapped her from him. But if these silent pleas had
   meaning, maybe neither knew.
The girl child's only comfort came from nestling under the
   lychee tree. Its shifting branches
whistled her wordless lullabies: the lychees with their watchful eyes,
   the wild geese crossing overhead.
The fruit, the geese. They marked her seasons. She didn't long to join
   the birds, if longing implies

a will beyond the blindest instinct. Then one mid-autumn, she craned
          her neck so far to mark the geese's
wheeling through the clouded hills – it kept on stretching – till
          it tapered in a beak. Her pink toes
sprouted webs and claws; her helpless arms found strength
          in wings. The goose daughter
soared to join the arrowing skein: kin linked by a single aim
          and tide, she knew their heading

and their need. They spent that year or more in endless flight,
                                        but where –
          across what sparkling tundral wastes –
I've not heard tell. Some will say the fable ended there. But those
          who know the ways of wild geese
know too the obligation to return, to their first dwelling place.
                                        Let this
          suffice: late spring. A woodsman
snares a wild goose that spirals clean into his yard – almost like
          it knows. Gripping its sinewed neck

he presses it down into the block, cross-hewn from a lychee trunk.
          A single blow. Profit, loss.

Frenzied

Maybe holding back
is just another kind

of need. I am a blue
plum in the halflight.

You are a tiger who
eats his own paws.

The day we married
all the trees trembled

as if they were mad –
be kind to me, you said.

Innumerable

Poem on the eve of May 35th

In the early summer of 1989, when I was five, my parents took me on an unusual outing. It wasn't that the Jockey Club's track in Wan Chai (at that time still epitheted 'Royal') was unfamiliar to me: every week I went there for an hour's swimming lesson in the too-hot pool, my reward an orange ice lolly from the freezer cabinet behind the clubhouse bar. But I knew things were different that Saturday. For one I had never stepped on the actual grass before. On race days, that was the preserve of the slow processing row of black-trousered labourers, their cone hats and canes, who would follow on after the rumbling of the horses – their job, with a practised touch as of the blind, to feel out the slightest hoof-flung sod and tamp it back into the reperfected turf. I spent the day hoisted on my father's shoulders, staring out across the jellied mass of human heads. On the big screen, the dots of light weren't tickering the customary shifting dance of odds, but the exact words, Chinese then English, that would reverberate from the ten thousand mouths held in the stadium's bowl, as the crest of skyscrapers stood watch. On the news that evening I tried to pick out my waving self among the banners' swell, the toybox people chanting and abuzz. A few days later there were different pictures on the news. A man with two white shopping bags edging crabwise on a faceless boulevard in another city where twenty-three years later I would struggle for over half an hour to hail a cab. On rainy race days the turf workers, still bamboo-brimmed, would wear transparent macs dotted with drizzle and the determination of a search party. Where they pressed the clumps back down, you would never know.

73

Others

I think about the meaning of *blood*, which is (simply) a metaphor;
and *race*, which has been a terrible pun.

*

From *castus* to *chaste*, with a detour for *caste*.
English, 廣東話, Français d'Egypte, עמאמ - יִשְׂאָל: our future children's
    skeins, carded.

*

A personal Babel: a muddle. A Mendel?
Some words die out while others survive. *Crossbreed. Halfcaste.
    Quadroon.*

*

Spun thread of a sentence:... have been, and are being, evolved.
The spiralling path from *Γένεσις* to *genetics*. Language revolves
    like a ream of stars.

*

A different generation: They wouldn't escape by the *Mischlinge Laws*.

I wonder if they'll have your blue eyes.

*

My Carol Service reading on the seed of Abraham: tittering.

The *sand which is upon the seashore* had made them think of a picnic lunch.

廣東話 – *Guangdong wah*: 'Cantonese (language)'.

עמאמ - וְשָׁאל – *mame-loshn* – 'Yiddish' (literally 'mother tongue').

Having just broken the water pitcher

Baizhang picked up a water pitcher, set it on a rock, and posed this question: 'If you cannot call it a water pitcher, what do you call it?'

WUMEN HUIKAI, *The Gateless Gate* (13th Century)

This fact I can't forget: my thirtieth year
had hastened by before I learned to see
how *plum blossom* lies one sidelong stroke   梅

of gum-suspended soot away from *regret*.   悔
It's said the man who invented writing
charged with this burden by the emperor

sought inspiration in the surface moods
of water; that he was by the river
when he spied in the finely cracking mud

a hoofprint, its brim still as a bronzed mirror,
stamped there by some invisible creature –
and understood his task. The moment he sketched

the first character, the sky rained millet
and the ghosts wailed all night for they could not
change their shapes. Five thousand years later

in some remote coalmining district sits
an anonymous blogger, his face lit
by more than just the ancient monitor.

He ponders how strange it is (how useful...)
that *I beg you for the truth* is pronounced
the same as *I beg you, Elephant of Truth!*

Or that *sensitive words* (as in filters,
crackdowns) sounds exactly like *breakable
porcelain*. Done typing, he clicks *Submit*.

Recall the old monk's koan, the correct
reply to Master Baizhang's question:
His pupil kicked over the pitcher and left.

That from a long way off look like flies

More a midge really, flower-pressed: pent
        in this hinged spread of my *Riverside Shakespeare*.
Two thousand translucent sheets not the worst
        of cerements. Down the page, a grey smudge.
Tinged with a russet penumbra, like blood –
        mine or its? One wing, not quite glimmering,
curves like a glyph in a strange alphabet.

Flattened in some far Holy text, a fly's
        errant diacritic, shifting the sense,
might launch a war for a millennium.
        Caught in here, it turns a mawkish moral:
how viewed down a long enough corridor
        Death can be unfelt, mean, ridiculous
and true. When Titus goes berserk, the joke

is empathy's mirror: *how, if that fly*
        had a father and mother? On the heath,
Lear assumes all ragged madmen must have
        ungrateful daughters. The way my father
in his affable moods, thinks you always
        want a gin and tonic too. I wonder
if I should scrape her off with a tissue.

INUA ELLAMS

■ **INUA ELLAMS** was born in Nigeria in 1984. He lives in and works from London as a poet, playwright, performer, graphic artist and designer. He has toured with the British Council to Libya, Nigeria, India, Australia, Malaysia, America, Bangladesh, Pakistan, New Zealand and Austria and is an experienced workshop leader. His published plays include *The 14th Tale* (flipped eye, 2010), which won a Fringe First Award at the Edinburgh Festival 2009 and ran at the UK's National Theatre, *Knight Watch* (Oberon), *Untitled* (Oberon), *Cape* (Oberon) and most recently another National Theatre production *Black T-Shirt Collection* (Oberon). Other works include *Wild Blood* (BBC Radio 3) and *The Ballad of Abdul Hafiz* (BBC Radio). His poetry is widely published, notably in *Thirteen Fairy Negro Tales* (flipped eye), *Candy Coated Unicorns and Converse All Stars* (flipped eye), the *Salt Book of Younger Poets* (Salt, 2011), *Mud Wrestling with Words* (Burning Eye, 2013) *Chorus* (MTV Books, 2012), *Waterfront* (Louis Vuitton), *The ScapeGallow* (Tate Modern) as well as *Magma* and *Wasafiri*.

Inua describes himself as an immigrant – nationally, internationally, digitally and artistically – and these various spaces gave rise to the Midnight Run, an event where he combines his search for place and belonging with members of the wider public. To date, he has held Midnight Runs in Milan, Florence, Barcelona, Manchester and London. ■

■ W.N. HERBERT:

Inua Ellams' work juxtaposes with the easy grace of the born storyteller the fraught but still fantastic realm of formative myth – 'Of all the boys of Plateau Private School' – with the more testing times of maturation, in which the psyche comes to terms with its own moral standards and the social niceties and political necessities of the society it matures into.

These are particularly tales of masculinity, with its attendant crises of peer rivalries and relationships defined through the physicality of sport, the command of that coded sort of knowledge which defines what is cool, as well as being marked by violence and defiance of authority.

What distinguishes his vision is a strong sense of the paradoxical link between the intensities of youth and the obsessions of adulthood: how closely the desire of the one to be seen as adult is linked to the hubristic immaturity of the other. That our role models, idealised as superheroes by the child, usually turn out to be no better than their more mundane secret identity – if not something worse – may seem like a melancholy rite of passage, but it is told with wit and gusto in these poems. The poet understands that such processes are performed rather than understood: we act out our desires, and so come to uneasy terms with them.

Add to this an impressive grasp for detail and dialogue, capturing the very different milieus of the UK and Nigeria, and we realise these narratives are also a metaphor for the way in which societies and their religions read and misread each other, idealising or condemning that which they are in the act of becoming or attempting to separate themselves from.

These are poems about growing up, which evoke youth and cultivate a youthfulness of voice, but they already contain an impressive maturity of insight into the joys and pitfalls of that most necessary and forever incomplete activity. ■

Of all the boys of Plateau Private School,

the dry-skinned short shorted dust-dipped
            disciples of Bruce Lee and Chuck Norris,
of all the wire-headed heathen, my posse
            of Voltron-Forced, Fraggle-Rocked,
Teenage Mutant Hero Nerds each had a party trick.
            Kika B would eat a fist-full of desert sand
spiced with soldier ants, chew till it turned
            the beige mulch of Rich Tea biscuits,
swallow twice, and live to tell the tale.
            Dapo Mokoye could flatulate the first line
of the national anthem with such clarity,
            Raymond Ogunsayo swore he heard words.
T could spit faster than fleas skip, further than
            lizards leap, spit so high, we claimed him
Herculean in form, a half-god of rainfall
            and of the four talents, I was the art kid
awaiting the school bell.

With the sun for floodlights, the ground
            for canvas, a sharp twig splashing
sand about like paint, I'd capture Kika's grin,
            Dapo's musical sin, T's thick lips
saliva dripping and me, angled as a
            Ghetto van Gogh; shoulders hunched
to get the staunch slouch right. We'd pose beside
            the drawing, sculptures of ourselves,
the other boys clustered, dark eyed, envious but
            not enough to scatter sand in any way.
So this day after, we sidle into school, still
            sketch-slouched, find our canvas suddenly

blank, sand – mysteriously smoothed…
       Most likely the caretaker simply did his job,
but instead we imagine creatures of the night,
       voodoo priests and priestesses, mami waters,
bush babies, witch doctors, sorcerers,
       all the sulphur-scorched, glowing-eyed
-black-circled venom stuff rumoured to work
       the night, we theorise they spent
their witching hour playing with our sand.

The priest outlined us in white chalk, spoke
       in voodoo talk, raised up dust dolls of us
who, naked with the witches, limboed with
       their brooms; bush babies gaggled
and gooed in devil-glee till the clock struck three,
       they vanished instantly, a foul wind
of howling wolves swept through, leaving sand
       smooth as fresh sheets, as the wide ruled page
I dent and reminisce of tongues turned tireless,
       of dark art's thrill, of how quick we fixed
our lil' plight with fantasy, which flows,
       you know, ever shapes, ever reveals
the world to whoever asks it, some trap it
       with tongues or a double bass strummed,
some turn its incline to sculpted forms, a boy
       once enticed it with sand and a stick
or now, as I do, with a pad and a Bic.

Short Shorted / Odogbolu 1995

All this is fact /

That Jebo had a knack for melodrama.
That his slight weight barely marked
That boarding school ground.
That he was teased for his fair complexion.
That he'd skim most crowds in search of me.
That his left arm crowned my shoulders so often
That some thought us more than good friends.
That we walked to dormitories after classes.
That we were gathered out in the cold courtyard.
That we were lectured on theft and property.
That Balla was nabbed with bags of stolen food.
That our knees knocked in our short shorts.
That a storm roared over the fields.

All this is feasible /

That Balla was Goliath to Jebo's David.
That a visible tension lay between them.
That Balla ate rice laced with rocks.
That these were the building blocks of his muscles.
That once he picked a senior clean off the floor.
That we called him Spartacus, a hero to us.
That Balla wasn't guilty of theft.
That he was too thick to master such things.
That the prefect chose the toughest canes.
That lashes flashed down with such force
That Balla could make no sound at all.
That Balla chose to make no sound.

84

That the prefect so hated his show of strength
That he broke two canes across Balla's back.
That another ripped a cable off the wall.
That its sparks hugged air for a second.
That he touched this to Balla's wet skin.
That Balla shook like a bird on fire.
That Jebo smiled when Balla screamed.
That Balla broke free, ran for a window.
That the search party never found him.

All this is fiction /

That I pulled Jebo's arm off my shoulder.
That I joined those who taunted him.
That Balla lost all diction that night.
That when he landed, he ran for the mountains.
That the storm struck the last of our Titans.
That often when lighting strikes those fields
instead of thunder, something / someone screams.

Ghetto van Gogh

The night my mother tells the story of the thief, I am cross legged on her lap. Her mouth is inches from my ear. She lets the dusk slip into her voice and whispers about the boy who snatched a mango at the market and ran, becoming the teen-ager who robbed a shop at gun point, shot the blind cashier, shot him as he fell, shot him once more dead; became the man who stole 36 cars and when apprehended, to be publicly hanged, asked for one wish, his whole lip quivering.

My mother, who is inches from my ear, explains his dying wish to speak to his mother. The silent crowd parted, she gathered his bound wrists to her lips, kissed his rough skin, her cheeks shimmering in the killing heat. He bent forward, my mother says, her mouth even closer, her dusky voice hushed, bent forward as if to kiss her cheek goodbye and switched sharply, bit into her ear, strained against the flesh, ripped the thing off and spat you should have told me mother, what I did was wrong.

Swallow Twice /

Given the smallest prompt, Father will describe
how I skulked just beyond the lamplight's reach

watching the ring of men ripe with beer and laughter
push thick fingers into the mountain of spiced meat

roasted with onions, ginger and chillies like an altar
I fought to worship at, swiping through their arms

at the chunks – a mouse attempting to feast with kings.
Frustrated, Father stopped their speech

so I could reach in, greedily choose the choicest piece,
ignore his warnings and tear at the muscle, strain

against the flesh till its elasticity slipped my fingers
and the chunk, chillies and all slapped into my eyes.

Father thumped my back as I coughed on the pepper
/ swallow twice he urged / dropping the wailing mess

of me on Mother's knees. What Father didn't know
is I imagined the key to their impenetrable talk

lay in the cubed meat and I longed to be like them.

In the circle of friends I have, most of our conversations
revolve around music, the heft and sway of the changing

world, the rapid rate of our redundance, how best
to pretend we know it all and when beer loosens

what inhibitions are left after shredding meat
with bare fingers, laughter cloaks our weaknesses:

our inabilities to provide for those we love, who love us,
we who still know nothing of what our lovers want,

how frightening it is to be have nephews growing up
who want to be like us, like men.

Swallow twice, and live.

When I say Wez towered over us, I mean
the last oak in a forest of stumps, a lighthouse
glowing over beached ships, a steeple in a valley
of slums,we were dwarfed by this fabulous animal
who howled to Master P and DMX, bouncing
on his toes, a wolverine glint to his eyes, a vicious
wild I once saw unleashed against a better team,
seconds on the shot clock and all to play for.

The next time I saw Wez desperate, he had tired
of the threat to his throne of tallest baller to roam
the school's gym. Let me set the scene: an empty court,
a light quarrel on Nas lyrics or chicken sandwiches
and Rooney, the rival giant has Wez headlocked.
There's a dip, something copied from a Bruce Lee flick.
Wez twists to fling the whole entire bulk of his weight
against Rooney, misses his mark and is struck down.

When I say Wez broke his shoulder blade, I mean
an ancient tree toppled in a forest, a leviathan rose
from the deep, a bible split down its middle, a slow
motion shock spread from the splintering, hushed
us all and we wondered if he'd blubber? Would
he crack? Die of embarrassment? Wail as kids do?
Or swallow the gathering sob about his eyes?
Swallow again, if that's what it took?

The National Anthem

The mango seed
(you hid in the left corner
under the grand piano
in the back room of the house
in which you were born
on the corner of Joy Avenue
in a warm suburb overlooking
a highway's traffic
chugging north toward the airport
for long distant flights over
choppy waters, sail boats, yachts
and ocean liners now silhouettes
in the picturesque sunset
where you land and taxi out
to cold, snow-slushed streets
of grey neighbourhoods
and slim buildings
creaking with metal stairs
and small apartments tight
as veins you want to pry open
on the damp bedroom floor
in the right corner
where the keyboard tinkles out
our national anthem)
will still grow when you return.

The / Forced

One day when you are pissing on the roadside,
your cracked bare feet on grass streaked with faeces
and purewater plastic bags, you will hear his name
and turn to watch his convoy numerous as the aunts,
the uncles and ancestors you have never known, inch
down the crowded Mushin street singing his praises
as if a capitalist black Jesus, dishing cold hard cash
to those pressed either side of his jeep, hands out –
stretched, pleading with a hunger you know too well.

One month later, when another born-troway smoking
stolen indian hemp talks softly of the crude oil rags
and patchwork dishcloths you both wore as nappies,
shivers from the same foul breeze blowing the truth
of your fractured life, you will call his name, Oluomo,
speak its solid weight and wonder if it is worth a try.

One year after your quick slim fingers have caught
the attention of his boys who dance drunk on paraga,
the oil drum fire flickering in their eyes, you will hear
they too were born and thrown away, they had snakes
for mothers too, but were lifted from gutters and now
are this city-wide tribe of hard men spidering through
the night Oluomo alone controls: homes raided, rivals
knifed, politicians bribed, the rich ransomed and each
area-boy willing to die for each. You marvel at such
family, ask if they need help, anything you will do.

One decade from now, when police who are vicious
as they are duplicitous have beaten you senseless,
have dumped your swollen self in a concrete cell,
when you deny them the satisfaction of betrayal
/ no be by force o, it wasn't by force / you will cry
your throat dry as cracked feet, sob uncontrollably
as blood bubbling your torn nostril bursts, you will
call for your brothers, but for now you are free.

EDWARD DOEGAR

■ **EDWARD DOEGAR** was born in Surrey, grew up in Hull and now lives in London. He studied English at Nottingham and spent a year in South Carolina. His poems and reviews have appeared in various magazines including *Poetry Review*, *Poetry London*, *Magma* and *Ambit*. He is the General Manager of the Poetry Society. ■

■ SEAN O'BRIEN:

In 'The Waiting Room', a family endures uncertainty about the father's recovery from an operation. In this stalled meantime, 'yawns are a guilty pleasure, / sharing the contagious privacy of the body': the language is characteristic of Edward Doegar in its combination of lucidity and richness. The poem's ancestry lies in the stern self-scrutiny of Robert Lowell's *Life Studies*: 'I try to ration the thrill of being / almost orphaned.' Doegar is a moralist, interested in what constitutes right action and in the ways in which temperament, history, luck and the permanent compromise of family life may obstruct it. I think this makes him fairly unusual among contemporary poets. For Doegar, the world and its various forms of order – family, religion, politics, ethnicity, gender, marriage – have to be reckoned with, rather than subjected to an indolent irony which has already made up its mind that it knows everything.

It's likely that Doegar would agree with Pound's description of technique as a test of sincerity. Doegar's poems have a sense of scrupulous clarification, for example, as in 'Something Understood' (a title taken from George Herbert's definition of prayer), where the urge to dismiss belief is balanced with the urge to share it and with the impossibility of deciding between two courses: 'Forgive / us our trespasses / How many mouths has it mattered to? / How many has it fed? / Enough. Find the light, the door. Be sated.' The closing rhyme, where unstress is matched against stress, is, as it were, in debate with the full rhymes employed earlier in the poem – the kind of beautifully carpentered detail that underwrites Doegar's compelling seriousness about what the art of poetry may be able to accomplish when musicality and insight are wedded. ■

Half-Ghazal

(for Reneé)

> *The word [Ghazal] is of Arabic origin and means 'talking to*
> *women' (women in purdah, with all that that implies)*
>
> MIMI KHALVATI in her notes to *The Meanest Flower*

I flinch inside as you corroborate my name,
which is your name

now. You spell it out over the phone to a call centre
in India. Your new surname

as foreign to you as the phone-wallah
at the other end. Though the name

itself was born and bred in the Himalayas,
in Hindi, it's long been reformed into English, into the name

you now pronounce
in your own, non-native, North American. It's a name

you'll freely admit you'd rather not have taken
but have taken all the same, exchanging one unchosen name

for another, uncasting yourself as Kohanim.
And yes, I was proud you agreed to bear my name,

to belong to my skin,
to share the cloth of my sisters' maiden name.

But now, as you get used to an alias, I recall
my mother, who wouldn't disown her married name,

but lived with it, assimilated, as my father's
ex-wife, determined to keep the same last name

as me. You begin again: *Dee – Oh – Eee – Jee – Ay – Arr*
and I blush at the burden of our name.

Consent

A few hours in and we're still stuck on adultery,
Agreeing
About the unread Qur'an and its criminal bigotry,
Citing the Commentary page in the paper:
How men, my age, will fling
Stones at a girl because they'd like to rape her.

The Waiting Room

Three hours of snow but nothing's settled.
We've a routine on the weather: the door opens,
automatically, to deposit the punch-line.
Our fluorescence ticks…
Timing, as they say, is everything. We lope together
to the coffee machine, stuck on the instant.
I borrow a second cigarette from the cleaner
who coughs, in English, about the cost of cigarettes.
My brother-in-law returns with a fleece.
Conversation's slow, as if words were the last
chocolates left in the box. The air rings with *If…*
A poster lists the tell-tale signs of a stroke,
how Face, Arms or Speech will fall
in the fight against Time. But the acronym annoys,
here everything stalls: yawns are a guilty pleasure,
sharing the contagious privacy of the body.
We try to draw our thoughts from a conclusion.

*

The scribble of hair on his chest glistens,
a clutch of seaweed washed up on the sand.
My father lies on a coral carpet, chin bent
to his chest, beached at the foot of the bed.
He tries to hold his breath between breaths,
counting each one in. When he speaks
he looks past me as if reading the wallpaper.
His pyjama shirt drifts open, then open further
as he asks what time it is again. In the en-suite
a colossal drip reverberates in the tub,
Co. Cork's own water torture…

He concentrates on something, it's nearing
like a tennis ball. I am no longer there.
Then his hand takes mine – an arm-wrestle,
unexpectedly firm, it clenches and deflates.
Instructions becoming suggestions becoming
descriptions…

*

Through the locked glass door, the corridor
dwindles to a twitching bulb – a light
at the end of the tunnel. Humour narrows
to the inevitable. We keep each other awake
taking shifts as the driver, the passenger.
Outside the snow has given up the ghost;
it's clear, still, my breath clouds like smoke.
The car park is bathed in slow amber syrup.
It is 03:44 am. It is 03:46 am.
No one else is waiting with us tonight.
In a small city like this, fewer people die.
I'm tired of such profundity. A whisper passes
through a pane of glass, the shiver of attention
lifts us. We stand, ready ourselves for a scene
but everyone looks out of costume
except the nurse. We wait behind the glass
trying not to over-rehearse the grief.

*

My thigh sticks to the seat, twenty years before,
a Summer in school shorts, Iron-Bru bars…
A nurse clicks towards us, the patterned echoes
of cardiology, that first inappropriate itch
of uniformed desire. I move my Latin homework
over my lap, continue declining no one's advances

Amo, amas, amat… The nurse clicks past.
Descending from my mother down, the family sits,
nervous and bureaucratic, a sub-committee
with nothing to report on, while a specialist
is cross-examined inside. The coming conference
can wait. For an hour we've been exercising
our single imagination – pressing at the fresh scab
of his survival. I try to ration the thrill of being
almost orphaned, of being kept off-school.
My mother tends a hysteric calm, correcting
my conjugations. I must concentrate hard.

*

He asks me how I am. The sun keeps wincing
behind a huge lumbering cloud. This is the future.
We talk about the garden, a row of pansies
he's planted. The brim of his panama hat
turns slowly through his gentle fingers
like the wheel of a car. He manoeuvres
into each conciliatory question
with an endless patience. Ice cubes rattle
up and down my glass. The teak sun loungers
have weathered to the colour of cement.
From inside the house we hear his grandson
using the Xbox to learn how to swear.
'Your nephew takes after you, I think.'
We both smile. He says he's proud
of the re-potted acer tree. He asks me
how I am. I tell him I'm fine. I tell him
all my adult life I've been writing his elegy.

Something Understood

Be seated. So much silliness. Go in fear
    of imperatives. Love,
as much as anything else, as little.
    Stop trying to touch
the stained light, it's not for you. Feel
    the wood instead; use
has polished the grain, this is not good,
    this is not evil. Wood
is also stained. And so on. Deliver us
    from this, from that.
From our petty convictions. Is it true
    that belief makes
something true? If only here? If
    only. Listen: the hinge
of restlessness caught in a pew, a child
    itching to join in. Give
us this day our daily bread. Forgive
    us our trespasses.
How many mouths has this mattered to?
    How many has it fed?
Enough. Find the light, the door. Be sated.

April

(after Li Po)

God has forgiven me again

The wind taps at the blinds
A tethered boat

On the fridge a reminder
To pick up milk

I step from the porch into rain
A blessing

Today even the gutter-water
Will be fresh

That Elegiac Tone

At the station bench, waiting for the London train, my father points to the wasteland across the way saying, as the sun comes out, 'I prefer that to a garden – those little scrubs, those weeds and grasses...' and it moves me, that he's so moved, moves me to claim the preference too, to praise the contrast of dock leaves and concrete, to liken it to an early Dürer etching; but it seems to annoy him, my interest in it, as if by trying to share in his sincerity I were being unkind, ungenerous, and as he stands up to turn his mind to the train, delayed now from Stansted, he utters only his simple 'No', a quiet corrective, while I go on thinking – 'what is a wasteland then? what makes it so? and why, if he likes it, shouldn't I?' But only words come back, only the neat debris of poems: shadowy red rocks and clutching roots; that vase; a whole century of dust on the nettles.

RISHI DASTIDAR

■ **RISHI DASTIDAR** was born in London and educated at Mansfield College, Oxford University and the London School of Economics. A graduate of the Faber Academy and a member of Malika's Poetry Kitchen, his poems have been *published by The Delinquent, The Poor Press, Tate Modern, Verbatim Poetry, Days of Roses, The Great British Bard-Off, Poems in Which, Dog Ear, And Other Poems, Poetry Digest, The Brautigan Book Club* and *Cake* magazine, amongst others. He was a runner-up in the 2011 Cardiff International Poetry Competition, and featured in the 2012 anthologies *Lung Jazz: Young British Poets for Oxfam* (Cinnamon Press and Eyewear Publishing, 2012) and *Adventures in Form* (Penned in the Margins, 2012). ■

■ DALJIT NAGRA:

Rishi is one of those rare things – a natural poet. Poems appear on the page with no residual trace of the sweat and strain that endless revising can impose upon the final version. He has a verbal fluidity, an astonishing range of references, a technical ease and a persistent imaginative surprise, often surreal, that makes his work feel fresh and contemporary. His tones vary from the deadly serious to the tongue-in-cheek and he often makes great emotional journeys within a poem.

Rishi's highly affecting love poems dare to be heartfelt but without being sentimental or simply earnest. They capture the tone of lived experience and are always true not so much to the decorum and tropes of traditional verse as to the genuine sentiments arising from a dramatised context. He is also a very skilled and sophisticated satirist who eschews direct outrage preferring instead an undercurrent of sorrow, a sense of loss to help us consider the wrong turn taken.

Although Rishi comes from an Indian background his poems are not limited by the culture. Nor are his influences, which incorporate the wit of the Metaphysical poets and the stylish excess of the New York poets. He is also highly know-ledgeable, not only about poetry, but about a wide range of subjects ranging from pop music, football, theatre, economic theory and the complex workings of a computer. Thankfully, as with his poetry, he carries this learning lightly. ■

Licking stamps

Let me guess, painter boy. You'll depict me
as your Emma Hamilton in that Romney portrait,
all cheesecloth and Circe,
before moving to some nonsense
about how I'm an antebellum babe
and that you have a battleplan for courting
to neuter my gattling gun tongue.
And then you'll have me say something
like, 'I want to be ravaged like Dresden
in 1945', when clearly I want to be
ravaged like Northumbria in 865.
But still, really, the martial metaphor?
I don't want things like 'fireworks'
or 'starlight' either. The oil spill is better,
but then that's making sex with me
topical when it should be newsworthy.
I know, I've got it. How about:
fucking me is like licking stamps?
Sticky, time consuming and capable of
taking you to destinations exotic and
mundane. Yes, I like that very much.

22 March, Working in an Office
on Berners Street

It is four days and half an average lifetime
after a simile happened to Richard Brautigan

elsewhere, half an ocean away.
Nothing has happened to me

except that the sun has come out
for the first time in my life,

the way the light comes on when you open
a fridge, and two slices of last night's pizza

are waiting to be breakfasted upon.
In 38 years time, the Met Office and the news app

won't be able to tell you what happened but trust me,
it's as true as the expression on your face right now.

The British genius

isn't for financing things or inventing games,
teaching them to others, playing them fairly
and badly and still turning up. No, it's actually
all the conversation, the hot air if you like,
that powers everything, anything of worth
(note, not of value) that we do. All those lawyers,
advertisers, politicos, pundits, journos,
stuttering aristos, dare I say it poets too;
what do you think they run on? The charm,
the listless seduction, where do you think they
come from? You know why the shipping forecast
is the nation's secular hymn? It's not for sailors;
it's for those in the navy of hyperbole, so they
know where to find it, to get their sails refilled.

Making a cheese soufflé rise

David Ogilvy is swashbuckling opposite me,
wreathed in the blue smoke

of his success. His expression says,
'Do not think that advertising is not a job for you,

that you are too proud to sell.
I burnt my hands in kitchens

in Paris, France, and sir I can tell you
these acts of persuasion

you undertake are nothing
compared to making

a cheese soufflé rise
under the gaze

of an elite brigade you can never join.
And once you are done

examining your navel remember
this is a noble calling,

alerting the world, waking it up.
You are the messenger of a good thing,

whatever your Frankfurt School says,
and that is a worthy thing for any man

who calls himself a man.
Now, then. Go. Rise. Work.

Towards a singularity

The appointment was 5pm,
outside of our normal hours.
She arrived in the King's Arms
wearing a leopard print coat like armour,
clutching a white handbag shield.
Her weapon was heartfelt logic;
my whisky rapier had no response,
bent out of the shape by the words
'it will never happen'.
The gap was filled by two physicists,
talking about the end of time.

Talking about the end of time,
the gap was filled by two physicists –
'it will never happen'.
Bent out of shape by the words,
my whisky rapier had no response.
Her weapon was heartfelt logic.
Clutching a white handbag shield,
wearing a leopard print coat like armour,
she arrived in the King's Arms
outside of our normal hours.
The appointment was 5pm.

Gunmetal

(for Ian E)

The sky vibrates like Mussolini's mistress's dentures in a
    Waterford tumbler
The sky throbs precipitately pink, like the ululating oestrogen
    of a Take That fan
The sky is a precious, precious green Edmund, a precious,
    precious green
The sky is as cold as a week-old gazpacho made out of tinned
    tomatoes
The sky is as playfully obtuse as an obscure collection of
    Flaming Lips B-sides
The sky is as rigorously gloomy as a Bank of England
    economic forecast
The sky is an edition of *Noel's House Party*: full of gunge, and
    the sound of a booming God laughing at our pratfalls
The sky is a flying change of leg in the dressage
The sky is a Tao Lin Google Chat, endlessly referring to its
    own digital circularity
The sky is not the sky: it is the sea, having got terribly
    confused at JobcentrePlus
The sky is an engine, powered by steam and onions and
    polystyrene chips
The sky is just fucking awesome, ok, and doesn't need a
    weapons-based simile to make it so

KAYO CHINGONYI

■ **KAYO CHINGONYI** was born in Zambia in 1987, moving to the UK in 1993. He holds an MA in Creative Writing from Royal Holloway, University of London and works as a writer, events producer and creative writing tutor. His poems are published in a range of magazines and anthologies including *Poetry Review, Magma, Wasafiri, The Best British Poetry 2011* (Salt Publishing), *The Salt Book of Younger Poets* (Salt Publishing, 2011), *Out of Bounds* (Bloodaxe Books, 2012), *The World Record* (Bloodaxe Books, 2012) and in a debut pamphlet *Some Bright Elegance* (Salt Publishing, 2012). He represented Zambia at Poetry Parnassus, a festival of world poets staged by the Southbank Centre as part of the London 2012 Festival. He was recently awarded the Geoffrey Dearmer Prize and shortlisted for the inaugural Brunel University African Poetry Prize. ■

■ ANTHONY JOSEPH:

Kayo Chingonyi's work is characterised by precision and an almost clinical attention to detail, to the minimalist nuances of language. His work is emotionally dense, and its wordscapes reflect the refracted vision of an outsider, one who stands just inside of the liminal gap. This process of being inside and out produces work that operates at the interstices. In his poems, Chingonyi is concerned with making the poem perform itself, to create shapes in the ear and eye. His Zambian heritage is woven, subtly into the poems, between the lines one hears the breath of the poet, we feel his stare, share his anguish. A sense of exile is implicit in the work. There is also an elegant restraint to his poems. And whilst Kayo is willing to experiment with form and wordplay, he is perhaps at his best when a glimpse of catharsis occurs, when the voice breaks:

> Show me the flat that stinks of our sleeplessness; plans hatched
> in the whispers of small hours. I'm tired of this strength. I'll be the ex,
> kempt lawn, best suit, watching the white limousine as it drives away.
>
> ('How to Cry')

Integral to Chingonyi's approach is an exploration of what he calls 'the music of language'. Language to him is an open field, a place where inspiration can be found in an overheard conversation, a melody, even according to him, from 'a comment on a video on youtube.' Hence, like many poets, Chingonyi transforms the mundane and the ordinary, into verse. Nothing is exempt. In the long sequence of poems 'calling a spade a spade' one witnesses this multitudinous approach, as well as the poet's unflinching gaze:

> My agent says I have to use my street voice.
> Though my talent is for rakes and fops I'll drop

the necessary octaves, stifle a laugh
at the playwright's misplaced get me blud and safes.

('calling a spade a spade', 'Casting')

Chingonyi is as influenced as much by hip hop culture as by philosophies of semantic association. As he suggests:

'Writing is a way of being attentive to language at a time when we are in such a rush to generate content (news, status updates, facile conversation) that the grace of the well-made utterance becomes less and less important.'

This attention to the nuances of language, and to the relationship between sound and form produces, in Kayo's work, original rhythmic shapes. In the Alexandrine lines of 'The Room', for instance, we encounter lines which borrow from hip hop in their verbal attack, but which seem almost formal in their construction and vocabulary:

For the purist, hung up on tracing a drum break
to its source, acquired in the few moments' grace

before the store-clerk, thin voiced, announces closing time

('The Room')

Music plays an important role in this shaping. It is through music that the word, the basic element of experience, is shaped into something that transcends its function. That is the task, I suggest, of poetry. And this perpetual motion of capturing and shaping informs Chingonyi's poems. It is, perhaps the true meaning of what Pound meant when he suggested that 'great literature' was 'simply language charged with meaning to the utmost possible degree'.

Chingonyi is a poet who is alert to the very possibilities of poetry, and who possesses the ability to use and assemble seemingly disparate fragments of experience into cogent forms, producing work that rewards both the reader and the listener. ■

How to Cry

I'm going to fold at the knees one of these days, in the middle
of Romford Market, and weep like a child forced to choose
between sweets or cuddly toy; mum or dad. Though I keep
God in a small closed box, I'll prostrate myself outside Argos,
beating the cobbles with my palm till blood sings in my fingertips.
There, amid cockneys selling fish, *box-fresh from Billingsgate*,
tears will occur to eyes I thought cried out. I want to be set off
by our red brick university, its constellation of strange faces.
Show me the flat that stinks of our sleeplessness; plans hatched
in the whispers of small hours. I'm tired of this strength. I'll be the ex,
kempt lawn, best suit, watching the white limousine as it drives away.

The Room

when you sample you're not just picking up that sound,
you're picking up the room it was recorded in

ODDISEE

For the purist, hung up on tracing a drum break
to its source, acquired in the few moments' grace

before the store-clerk, thin voiced, announces closing time
it's not just the drummer's slack grip, how the hook line

swings in the session singer's interpretation,
or the engineer's too-loud approximation

of the MacGyver theme tune, it's that hiss, the room
fetching itself from itself in hiccups and spools.

Though there's a knack in telling a-side, from remix,
from test press that never saw the light of day

mere completists never learn a good song's secret;
air displaced in *that* room – the breath of acetate.

calling a spade a spade

I no longer write
white writing
yet white writing
won't stop writing me

THOMAS SAYERS ELLIS, 'My Meter Is Percussive

The N Word

I

You sly devil. Lounging in a Pinter script
or pitched from a Transit van's rolled-down window;
my shadow on this un-lit road, though you've been
smuggled from polite conversation. So when
a friend of a friend has you, poised, on his lips
you are not what he means, no call for balled fist,
since he's only signifyin(g) on the sign;
making wine from the bad blood of history.
Think of how you came into my life that day,
of leaves strewn as I had never seen them strewn,
knocking me about the head with your dark hands.

II

Pretty little lighty but I can get dark

MZ BRATT, 'Get Dark'

You came back as rubber lips, pepper grains, blik
you're so black you're blik and how the word stuck to
our tongues eclipsing – or so we thought – all fear
that any moment anyone might notice
and we'd be deemed the wrong side of a night sky.
Lately you are a *pretty little lighty* who can
get dark because, even now, dark means street
which means beast which means leave now for Benfleet.
These days I can't watch a music video
online without you trolling in the comments
dressed to kill in your new age binary clothes.

Alterity

Our match maker, the only other *other*
kid in class, was my best friend after the urge
passed to slap your negritude out of his mouth.
Knowing what it was to have the spotlight
we stood in line for auditions in the hall.
In lieu of a third we were the two magi,
honouring a blue-eyed plastic messiah,
bearing our gifts of thrifty chinoiserie.
The holy mother was a girl named Phyllis.
I had my words down three weeks before the show:
'Come, Melchior; let's make the best of the light.'

The Cricket Test

Picture a cricket match, first week at upper
school, blacks versus whites, that slight hesitation
on choosing a side, and you're close to knowing
why I've been trying to master this language.
Raised as I was, some words in this argot catch
in the throat, seemingly made for someone else
(the sticking point from which all else is fixed).
We lost to a one-handed catch. After the match
our changing room was a shrine to apartheid.
When I crossed the threshold, Danny asked me why
I'd stand here when I could be there, with my kind.

On Reading 'Colloquy in Black Rock'

Just when I think I've shaken you off, you're there,
innocuous, in Lowell's poem – a flag
out of fashion, still flown by a patriot.
The seminar tutor tiptoes round you now.
Ours is to note the working mind behind the word
not what remains unsaid: there is us and them.
Cut to requisite dreads, beads, a wooden pendant
in the shape of a home I can't remember,
The Autobiography of Malcolm X.
Our first time alone together she asks
me why no one in my pictures is white.

Varsity Blues

An all-white production of *for colored girls*.
I expect my lecturer to get the joke
but he smiles, the thought of theatrical risk
becoming, in his mind, a piece in *The Stage*:
Drama student critiques our post-race moment.
I cast a banker's daughter from the second year
in the role of Tangie in spite of the minstrel-
show tone she affects to suggest otherness.
The student reporter praises the vision
of the production, the authenticity
of the performances, the light and shade.

Casting

My agent says I have to use my street voice.
Though my talent is for rakes and fops I'll drop
the necessary octaves, stifle a laugh
at the playwright's misplaced *get me*, *blud* and *safe*.
If I get it they'll ask how long it takes me
to grow *cornrows* without the small screen's knowing
wink. Three years RADA, two years rep and I'm sick
of playing *lean dark men who may have guns*.*
I have a book of poems in my rucksack,
blank pad, two pens, tattered A-Z, headphones
that know Prokofiev as well as Prince Paul.

* Clare Pollard, 'The Panther'

Callbacks

I have to stop working on my one-man-show
to take the call. They liked me, *but could I try
being Riley*, sotto voce, *the blind negro?*
When I got signed my agent told me *never
say no to good money*. She left out the part
about playing Sam in every room, itching,
of course, to play a tune. I take it, rent's due.
Besides, I would like to divide critical
opinion just once. I'll play him well-spoken.
My agent is elated. *That's great*, she says,
you're perfect for this role, you were born to play it.

Normative Ethics

In the safe distance of objectivity,
you can speak, with a straight face, of being
on the margins, being thought no longer *cool*
(if you don't know the curse that coolness confers):
women who prize your *chocolate voice* above
your words, or look at you like you've deserted
the cause because you are holding hands with your
pale-skinned lady. Men who tut like you've stolen
their birthright. A colleague, who doesn't see you,
angry at her own half-blackness, who cannot
believe her best friend is *fucking a nigger*.

JAY BERNARD

■ **JAY BERNARD** is from London and the author of two collections: *English Breakfast* (Math Paper Press, 2013), the result of a year as inaugural writing fellow at the National University of Singapore, and *Your Sign is Cuckoo, Girl* (Tall-Lighthouse, 2008) which was a PBS pamphlet choice. Jay's also an itinerant coder/zinester/graphic designer, and can be found at: jaybernard.co.uk. ■

■ KEI MILLER:

When a poet describing something so brutal as the aftermath of an execution, specifically a severed head placed on a spike, has both the freshness and the wildness of imagination to see in that piercing (the spike probably protruding from the head) something so extraordinarily disturbing and precise as the image of a tongue ('song to this spike that utters me'), then we know we are in the presence of a poet of significant powers. The startling image also provides us with one of the best metaphors for Jay Bernard's poetics, for her impulse is to observe and listen in to the braying crowd, to those who are celebrant and to those who are horrified and retching in the gutters, to the lawmakers and to the lawbreakers alike, and then to look at what rises like a monument from this crowd (the spike) and in imagining it as a tongue, as a thing in which language resides, she is attempting to coordinate and coalesce the voice of a crowd.

Bernard's heritage is Caribbean but this is a landscape she claims only insofar as it textures and transforms the dialect or urban Britain. Her own world is London in all of its messy multi-lingual, multi-dialectal, multi-racial, multi-sexual and relentlessly modern complexity. It is a dizzying milieu and a strange cacophony to try and utter with a single voice. Bernard doesn't struggle, as many younger poets might, to add complexity to her voice, or to experiment with new shapes, new modes, new metres for her poetry. It is her longstanding habit to do exactly that. She isn't a poet with a 'thing', in danger of plagiarising herself or flogging to death any horse she has chosen to ride. If anything, her problem is the opposite. So much is available to her and to her incredibly sharp and academic mind, that it is occasionally hard to distil, to hone in, to not become bored with a single direction. Alas, one must not come to Bernard's poetry looking for anything easy, or for a simple and unified vision. What she is very good at seeing is complexity. What she is very good at hearing is the cacophonous voice of the crowd.

I first met Jay four or so years ago at the StAnza poetry festival in Scotland. I was there for the week as Poet-in-residence; Jay was there as Artist-in-residence (it is her artwork that graces the cover of the present volume). Though she was, and indeed still is, quite young, having met her in a capacity that was the equal of mine I was a little surprised and fearful when asked in early 2013 to act as her mentor. There is little one can teach Jay Bernard. Quintessentially British in her refusal to draw attention to herself or her accomplishments, she is an Oxford-educated poet and artist who has held prestigious residencies in both the UK and abroad, completed a fair number of commissions and facilitated creative writing and art workshops to a large number of students. She thinks deeply about her craft(s) and the most musical, playful, and ethical ways to express the things she decides to express. If there is any single advice I have tried to give it is one which I fear, if taken too earnestly would be a disservice to the breadth of her talents – but it is to occasionally simplify, to now and again say it plainly, to sometimes strip back all the harmonies and recapture the melody of speech.

The poems here represent something of Jay Bernard's range. She is not a poet that can be easily reduced, boxed, summed up. Hers is a multiplicity of voices, and this is precisely her strength. The poems can be violent, raw, sexual, desperately intelligent – but at their best, always perfectly attuned to the young, urban crowd they find themselves in the midst of and rising from – something like a spike. Something like a monument. ■

Fake Beach

(for R.H.)

On St John's Island   you and your gay boyfriend
talked about beating up your ex.
It started with them   beating the shit out of you
and then it switched   to you beating the shit out of them.

Your gay boyfriend asked whether   people enjoy this
because they were slippered as kids   or because they weren't.
I thought of the   fucking/discipline   of parenthood
and how the rhythms aren't that different.

You've heard that bed-spring   and the flushing loo.
Your dad's stance   thigh muscles tight as he lowers
himself in   is the same   as when he draws back his arm.
He's as strong on your mother as he is on you.

You've heard that gasp   escape the hand pressed over it.
Seen possession   through a crack in the door-wood.
You've come back early to hear her   knock the side-lamp.
She loses it with him like she loses it with you.

We're drinking Tiger   on a fake beach   in Singapore.
Everyone burns in the water.   I'm under the umbrella
watching you   strong swimmer   go far out
flashing   arm-by-arm.

Don't they say   push the water away? Don't thrash.
Part the space   and enter it.

Song of the Strike

(FROM *The Back Swallow Stories*)

They carried me here when the strings of my muscles snapped.
The creak of the turning key made music
Of my body, and a voice that wasn't mine confessed.

                                   (the rest: ours too.)

When at a picture you stare, I am like the picture,
nude and narrative – I think I am the yellow-eyed
bust that you are; coloured statues watching the crowd.

                                   (the rest: us too.)

Where I once asked what statues speak of amongst themselves
now where I am I wonder what the people say
opening and closing their mouths on and around the air.

                                   (the rest: we too.)

They are upright with lightness – days like blowflies in their bellies,
the breath of each, hot in exchange with each,
and buoyant with each birthday.

Before I came to myself, I saw a colour like rotten breath.
Then I heard the sellers shouting out their wares.
When I came to, my head rested in my hand, hand atop chest.

I swivelled an eye and saw red in my sunward tilted lid,
And walking, elephants, without tusks, cart-driven carrion,
their insides slick to sauce; hawks circling on one-wing flight.
All the dismembered were there, all the dismembered were there.

There was no sky, there was no air. Everything as through
a peephole looked; no depth: the other creatures seemed so far away.

When they came close, small they remained.
Their smell raw, damp, high as a tanner's hand.

Below I saw a breath of bats swarm towards me,
swarming up towards me; below I saw their tiny bitter faces,
I heard through the still-tender pipes of my throat wing-hum,
clammy joints a-hum – coming up and through me –

And like starlings they veered right like thieves' eyes,
to be met by a grey light emerging from a point neither near nor
        far –
poultry-grey, hot and stinking – that god of my youth,
silent for twenty years, now spoke:

'As a matter of fact, I won't; as a matter of fact
you all hell-blown are born to serve in hell and so
in hell you'll remain. You protest in vain. Go back.'

And the swarm replied:

'Born to serve in hell, but born as angels were born,
And possessed of the same power of thought. Born,
and finding it difficult, frankly, to spend all eternity
with a spike in one hand, a woman's tongue in the other.
Give us a break, and make it fair to all who do work
that keeps the planes divided. There are many more
demons than angels and all of us are squat,
condemned, to stay life-after-life in torment
on the wheel of pointless toil. Do you know –
                         (God: 'I do.')
How difficult it is to saw a boy in half?
How our muscles turn to fetid mutton
striking pickaxes in the anuses of thieves?

131

How we sweat over the broth of shell-fish eaters,
mixed-wool wearers, prodigal sons?
And how hard to rest when the soulless beasts
of earth and air screech malformed, or when
a whale opens its jaws, beached on the ether
and fills this world with its stink?
Why us? If demons punish the wicked
we know better than angels do what is good –
and angels, clad in silk, would be devils
if they set foot on earth, so blinkered in their knowledge.'

There was a strike, thunder-like, like a hand-clap to the gnat
its echo was visible like sneeze-spray, each clap suspended
and terrible, and slow in motion. As each drop went by,
I heard/felt the smack of two unreal planes collide.
But the demons didn't move. With one voice they said:

'Here the bodies will stay wracked in hallucination,
and the smell will reach heaven, and we demons
will not cut or beat or burn or cruelly twist
or chop or flay or hang from digits, or fry another
until our argument is heard.'

Then they flew off. And one eye watched them go,
the other swivelled in its socket
and saw the crowd back at my hanging.
I heard my name, and when I looked to see
I saw the executioner laughing,
his fingers my insides interlaced – my stomach smelt of my
mother's cooking, suddenly, of my mother's cooking.

And when I turned again I was here, all of you beside me;
the crowd below, pausing, the river pausing,
song to this spike that utters me.

Punishment

I had this diary. A book with purple pages and gold keys.
One day I wrote in lilac pen that my mother was a bitch.
She found it and shook it at me. Shook the light gold keys
and purple pages, standing in her heels and fur coat.
Her hair, processed to black candy floss, was coming loose.
'Since you are so big,' she said, shaking the diary,
'let me remind you that it is my pussy you came from.'
She unbuttoned her coat, pressed my head against her thigh
and under her uniform skirt. Crinkle went the lining.
This, I thought, was better than the sharp slap I expected,
better than the sting of her spit as she screamed in my ear.
She pressed my head against her thigh and under her skirt,
ripping her tights, pushing aside her hot, damp knickers.
I closed my eyes and felt my forehead press against the familiar –
something like me, of looser spores, unexpectedly dry,
smelling of wet. '*Since you are so big*,' she said,
'let me remind you – ' and she told me with her body
that I was her child, a child, using cuss words I didn't comprehend.
Since you are so big, I was hearing the source of her voice,
no longer the breathy familiar but the root of that timbre,
the inner tom that hammered me into shape and sounded me out –
J-, J-, J- Jesus! With her ankles in the stirrups; J-, J-, J-
as she considered my name; and J-, and J-, and J-,
the far off edges of her voice, now a sound drying in a kiln.
Her heart is dark and clay, it's rhythm in the thick vein pressed
against my ear. I open my eyes and see the outside light below.
I see the inside of her knees through the tunnel of her thighs,
and hear my head slick against her insides as she grips me
for what will be the last time, grips me, screams and pushes me out.

Yes, they hate each other

My parents sleep beside each other and
they haven't spoken for a year.
They haven't spoken for a year and they sleep beside each other.
My parents haven't spoken and they sleep, wrapped together
in the same duvet though they haven't spoken for a year.
My parents do not speak, they don't meet eyes, but they sleep
in the same sweat, the same bundle, the same double bed.

The same bed I slept in when I crept in and crept in,
that bundle, that sweet heat, that warm double bed.
I don't know when I stopped or when I stopped or when I stopped
creeping in, and loving them and crying when they fought,
creeping in the bed that they slept in wrapped together,
foot against shin and shoulder to breast.

My parents sleep beside each other
and they haven't spoken for a year.
They haven't spoken for a year and they sleep beside each other,
When they once fucked and conspired about punishing us kids.
Now they sleep together, in the bed and the sweat of twenty years,
in this house, with its blind white windows, the cataracts of lace
in this south facing suburb, where the children play with fireworks,
the kids next door go missing, the babies are invisible,
the pickney dem go riding, the yout' all stand there smoking,
the students never visit, the schoolkids stab each other,
the young men start their families in their superhero bedsheets,
and my parents can be heard all caught up in their argument
By me and my brother and my sister and the street.

The Basics

In at least one staff toilet
someone is looking into the cistern
where the small pool of water –

and in at least one student toilet
someone is bunking a lesson,
trying to rub –

and upstairs in an empty classroom
a teacher begins to wonder
why it matters that –

while the widower cook in yellow gloves,
wipes the tables down
with two different kinds of –

then a parent sits up in bed
and screams at the teddies
lined up along the –

before kids from rival schools pile
onto a bus, cut their eyes at each other
and resist –

the careers advisor doesn't believe this girl
will amount to much, so scratches
her name from the –

in the park they put the day's lesson
to the test: the side of your eye is more
sensitive to light, so –

look to one side of a cluster you'll see it clearly;
like the stark younger face of your gran
if you barely –

The plough, or big dipper,
arching through the dark –
is not a funfair ride, but a question mark –

MONA ARSHI

■ **MONA ARSHI** is a poet, lawyer and mother. She was born and still lives in West London and has a Sikh Punjabi heritage. She initially trained as a solicitor and worked for the human rights organisation Liberty litigating cases under the Human Rights Act. She started writing poetry seriously in 2007 and completed her Masters in Poetry (Creative Writing) at the University of East Anglia with a distinction in 2013. She was first prize winner of the *Magma* Poetry Competition in 2011 and second prize winner of the Troubadour International Competition in 2013. Her poems have featured in magazines both in the UK and US. Mona has an interest in ghazals and Indian poetics. ■

■ MIMI KHALVATI:

Although born in West London, Mona Arshi was raised by Sikh Punjabi parents steeped in the culture of the East. Her father wrote ghazals and sang them during soirées with friends, while Mona passed round pistachios and poured the whisky. Later, she trained and worked as a lawyer and, perhaps rebelling against the language of the law, took up writing poetry four years ago.

Her early writing process was primarily through collage, harvesting striking images, looking for strange disjunctions, creative accidents, often with a surreal element. The disjunctive nature of the couplet in the ghazal, which Mona says is like a seeing a fresh drop of water and waiting till you see/hear the next drop, is perhaps what makes collage so natural to her. But more recently, she has also experimented with flow-writing, following an uninterrupted stream of thought and trusting in the images to arise from her memory bank organically. These contrasting creative processes have now fused and allowed her the freedom to draw on her innate versatility. Her range is already remarkable in the modes of lyric, prose poem, narrative, mythic retellings and now moving towards the sequence. Her tone ranges from the spare to the lush ("the sweetening stars"), the humorous to the elegiac. But whatever her mode, her distinctiveness is apparent and joyful, her originality stemming from an amalgam of influences: Donne, Heaney, Plath, Simic, Ghalib, Faiz, Lydia Davis, early Jorie Graham, Sujata Bhatt – a glorious mix of eclectic and benign assimilations.

Mona's hyphenated identity, her sometimes difficult subjects – the death of her brother, a family surviving loss, as well as more public themes – are seldom addressed head-on, but negotiated obliquely, sometimes slipping into gaps where she

139

finds the heartbeat, or residing in the minuscule – a bone in the ear, a grain of rice, eyelets in fabric, tiny objects which carry the unforeseen lightness of grief. ■

Ghazal

Not even our eyes are our own...
FEDERICO GARCÍA LORCA, *The House of Bernarda Alba*

I want to tune in to the surface, beside the mayfly,
listen to how she holds her decorum on the skin of the pond.

I want to sequester words, hold them in stress positions,
foreignate them, string them up to ripen on vines

and I want to commune with rain and for the rain
to be merciful, a million tiny pressures on my flesh.

I refuse to return as either rose or tulip but wish
to be planted under the desiring night sky,

concentrated to a line under the pleat of your palm
and for it to radiate opalesque under shadow.

I want God's fingers to break and for you to watch
as I fold my sleeve, reveal each detail of my paling wrist.

The Daughters

My daughters have lost
two hundred and thirty-six teeth
and counting.
They possess so many skills: they can
craft sophisticated weaponry such as blow-pipes,
lances and slings and know what the sharp end
of a peacock's feather is for.
Last month they constructed a canoe
and saved the *Purdu Mephistopheles* from extinction.
They may not know that a bird in the hand
is worth noting but have learned
never to bleed on any of the auspicious days
and are aware that pleasure
is a point on a continuum.
I fear they will never make good brides,
they are too fond of elliptical constructions
and are prone to lying in the dirt reading
paragraphs in the clouds.
Their shadows are long.
They know many things, my girls;
when they are older I will teach them
that abundance and vulcanisation
are bad words.
When they sleep, they sleep heavy;
I go into their rooms and check their teeth.

The Bird

She's a prize forager.
An assortment of beetle wings are arranged
like shiny badges under her bed.

Her meal worms have been freeze dried with such care
that they twitch in the bowl
when resurrected with just a speck of water.

She smells of ... preening oil, salt, top notes of earth.
My mother is turning bird.
This tiny impossible thing perched

in my hand,
molecules exciting her eyes.
Then the soft *click-click* that unlocks her humanity,

she separates from the tips of my fingers,
hops to the gap in the window,
leaving complex glitter in my palm.

Phone Call on a Train Journey

The smallest bone in the ear
        weighs no more than a grain of rice.

She keeps thinking it means something
        but probably is nothing.

Something's lost, she craves it
        hunting in pockets, sleeves,

checks the eyelets in fabric.
        Could you confirm you were his sister?

When they pass her his rimless glasses
        they're tucked into a padded sleeve;

several signatures later,
        his rucksack is in her hands,

(without the perishables),
        lighter than she had imagined.

In the Coroner's Office

Someone
is talking to me
about
my brother's body.

She doesn't know
in a certain light his
hair

took the colour of
blue-black ink
and how he would

wind himself
around my mother's body
to sleep.

She doesn't
know he was
born with
one

earlobe curled
tight
as a shell;
or how my mother
refused a doctor

and used
those first hours

to press
the new skin flat.

Notes Towards an Elegy

I

Entirely occupied. A million throats
migrate towards my ribs,
all pores and openings have acquiesced.
I'm slurring in my sleep.

II

The accumulation of departures,
mornings of staring down light.

Blame the bend in the trees.
Blame the abstract.
Blame my stupid dumb hands.

III

I've forgotten what silence feels like.
Tongue loosened with no protest,
my other tongue, a ceramic figurine,
presses against my teeth.

IV

What I know is that I'm straining to name the parts,
have failed to name the parts of the poem.

V

The back of my hand inscribed with dates
are like the hands of a small-boned boy
sitting under the twitching shade of a tree.

VI

We found the stumbling bird together
hand-fed her with white bread soaked in milk.

We had to leave her by the green shed and she did die.
You noted the delicate integrity of its fretwork.

VII

Wait fast ghost, you should see how
the living room is choked with living things
and your mother is sitting on your bed,
nurturing scraps in the poor light.

■ EDITOR'S BIOGRAPHY:

Karen McCarthy Woolf was born in London to an English mother and Jamaican father. She is the recipient of the Kate Betts Memorial Prize and an Arts and Humanities Research Council scholarship from Royal Holloway where she is a PhD candidate. Karen has taught creative writing widely, notably at the Southbank Centre, Photographers' Gallery, the Arvon Foundation, Poetry School and the environmental arts organisation Cape Farewell. She is the editor of two literary anthologies, *Bittersweet: Black Women's Contemporary Poetry* (The Women's Press, 1998) and *Kin* (Serpent's Tail, 2004) and is on the board of the international literary journal *Wasafiri*. Her poetry has been selected for Poems on the Underground, is published in *Prairie Schooner* as well as *Poetry Review* and *Modern Poetry in Translation*, both magazines for which she also reviews. She is a fellow of TCW I and her collection *An Aviary of Small Birds* is published by Oxford Carcanet in 2014. ■

■ MENTOR BIOGRAPHIES:

Patience Agbabi is a sought-after poet, performer and fellow in Creative Writing at Oxford Brookes University. She read English at Oxford University and has an MA in Creative Writing from Sussex University. Patience has spent over 20 years celebrating the written and spoken word. In 2004 she was nominated one of the UK's 'Next Generation Poets' for *Transformatrix* (Canongate, 2000). She has performed world-wide on British Council-sponsored projects and independent engagements including Glastonbury Festival, the Royal Albert Hall, Edinburgh Book Festival, Soho Jazz Festival and the Rough Talk Sweet Song tour of South Africa. Patience is active in the literature and arts scene and is on the Council of Management for the Arvon Foundation. Her collection *Bloodshot Monochrome* was published by Canongate in 2008. She was Canterbury Laureate from 2009 to 2010, and received a Grants for the arts Award to write *Telling Tales*, a contemporary version of *The Canterbury Tales* (Canongate, 2014).

Sasha Dugdale was born in Sussex and is a poet, playwright and translator. From 1995 to 2000, she worked for the British Council in Russia. She is author of the poetry collections *The Estate* (2007), *Notebook* (2003) and *Red House* (2011) and has translated Russian poetry and drama, including and Elena Shvarts's *Birdsong on the Seabed* (Bloodaxe Books, 2008) and Anton Chekhov's *The Cherry Orchard*. She has been editor of *Modern Poetry in Translation* since 2013.

Professor W.N. Herbert was born in Dundee, and educated at Brasenose College, Oxford, where he published his DPhil thesis (*To Circumjack MacDiarmid*, OUP, 1992). He established his reputation with two English/Scots collections from

Bloodaxe, *Forked Tongue* (1994) and *Cabaret McGonagall* (1996), followed by *The Laurelude* (1998), *The Big Bumper Book of Troy* (2002), *Bad Shaman Blues* (2006) and *Omnesia* (2013). His practical guide *Writing Poetry* was published by Routledge in 2010. He co-edited *Strong Words: modern poets on modern poetry* (Bloodaxe Books, 2000) with Matthew Hollis, and *Jade Ladder: Contemporary Chinese Poetry* (Bloodaxe Books, 2012) with Yang Lian. Born in Dundee, he is Professor of Poetry and Creative Writing at Newcastle University and lives in a lighthouse overlooking the River Tyne at North Shields.

Twice shortlisted for the T.S. Eliot Prize, his collections have also been shortlisted for the Forward Prize, McVities Prize, Saltire Awards and Saltire Society Scottish Book of the Year Award. Four are Poetry Book Society Recommendations.

Anthony Joseph is a poet, novelist, academic and musician. He was born in Trinidad, moving to the UK in 1989. He is the author of three collections of poetry and a novel, *The African Origins of UFOs* (Salt, 2006). In 2004 Joseph was selected by renaissance one, Decibel and the Arts Council of England as one of fifty Black and Asian writers who have made major contributions to contemporary British literature, appearing in the historic Great Day photo. In 2005 he was selected as the British Council's first Poet in Residence at California State University, Los Angeles. Joseph lectures in creative writing at Birkbeck College, University of London and holds a doctorate from Goldsmiths College.

As a musician he has released three critically acclaimed albums with his band the Spasm band; all released to coincide with book publications. His debut album with the band, Leggo de Lion was released in 2007, and featured lyrics taken from his novels, notably *Bird Head Son* (Salt, 2009).The band's third album *Rubber Orchestras* was released in 2011, alongside a new collection of poems with the same title. He has colla-borated with several artists including Archie Shepp, Joseph Bowie, Laurent Garnier, Othello Molineaux, Malcolm Catto, Mop Mop, Robert Aaron, Roger Raspail, Keziah Jones and Jerry Dammers of the Specials as part of the Spatial AKA Orchestra.

In 2012, Joseph represented Trinidad and Tobago at the Poetry Parnassus Festival on London's South Bank.

Mimi Khalvati was born in Tehran, Iran. She grew up on the Isle of Wight, where she attended boarding school from the age of six, and has lived most of her life in England. She trained at Drama Centre London and has worked as an actor and director in the UK and Iran.

She has published seven collections of poetry with Carcanet Press, including *The Meanest Flower*, a Poetry Book Society Recommendation, a *Financial Times* Book of the Year and shortlisted for the T.S. Eliot Prize and, most recently, *Child: New and Selected Poems 1991-2011*, a Poetry Book Society Special Commendation. Her work has been translated into nine languages and she received a Cholmondeley Award in 2006. She is a Fellow of the Royal Society of Literature. Mimi is the founder of The Poetry School and was the Coordinator from 1997 to 2004. She is a core tutor for the School and has co-edited its three anthologies of new writing published by Enitharmon Press.

She is also a freelance poetry tutor and has worked with arts organisations such as the Arvon Foundation and the Southbank Centre and has taught at universities in the UK, Europe and America.

Kei Miller was born in Jamaica in 1978. He read English at the University of the West Indies and completed an MA in

Creative Writing at Manchester Metropolitan University. *His work has appeared in The Caribbean Writer, Snow Monkey, Caribbean Beat* and *Obsydian III*. His first collection of short fiction, *The Fear of Stones*, was short-listed in 2007 for the Commonwealth Writers First Book Prize. His first poetry collection, *Kingdom of Empty Bellies* (Heaventree Press, 2006) was followed by *There Is an Anger That Moves* (2007), *A Light Song of Light* (2010) and *The Cartographer Tries to Map a Way to Zion* (2014) from Carcanet. He is also the editor of Carcanet's *New Caribbean Poetry: An Anthology* (2007). He has been a visiting writer at York University in Canada, the Department of Library Services in the British Virgin Islands and a Vera Ruben Fellow at Yaddo, and currently teaches Creative Writing at the University of Glasgow. In 2013 the Caribbean Rhodes Trust named him the Rex Nettleford Fellow in Cultural Studies.

Daljit Nagra was born and raised in west London and Sheffield by his Punjabi parents. He was awarded the Forward Poetry Prize for best single poem in 2004. His debut collection, *Look We Have Coming to Dover!* (Faber and Faber) was published in 2006 and won the Forward Prize for Best First Collection. He is also the author of *Tippoo Sultan's Incredible White-Man-Eating Tiger-Toy-Machine!!!* (Faber and Faber, 2011) and *Ramayana: A Retelling* (Faber and Faber, 2013). www.daljitnagra.com

Professor Sean O'Brien is a poet, critic, playwright, anthologist, novelist and editor. He grew up in Hull and now lives in Newcastle upon Tyne. He has published seven collections of poetry, including *Downriver* (Picador, 2007), *November* (Picador, 2011) and *Collected Poems* (Picador, 2012). His book of essays on contemporary British and Irish poetry, *The De-*

155

regulated Muse (Bloodaxe), was published in 1998, as was his acclaimed anthology *The Firebox: Poetry in Britain and Ireland after 1945* (Picador). His Newcastle/Bloodaxe Poetry lectures, *Journey to the Interior: Ideas of England in Contemporary Poetry*, were published in 2012. He has edited a selection from Andrew Marvell (Faber, 2011) and, with Don Paterson, *The Rest on the Flight: Selected Poems of Peter Porter* (Picador, 2010) and *Train Songs: Poetry of the Railways* (Faber, 2013). His collection of short stories, *The Silence Room*, appeared from Comma Press in 2008, and his novel *Afterlife* from Picador in 2009. He has translated Dante's *Inferno* and the poems of Corsino Fortes. His plays include *The Birds*, *Laughter When We're Dead* and *Keepers of the Flame*. His translation of Tirso de Molina's Spanish Golden Age comedy *Don Gil of the Green Breeches* was staged in 2013.

Pascale Petit was born in Paris, grew up in France and Wales and lives in London. She has published six poetry collections. Five poems from her latest collection *Fauverie* (Seren, 2014) won the 2013 Manchester Poetry Prize. *What the Water Gave Me: Poems after Frida Kahlo*, published by Seren in 2010 (UK) and Black Lawrence Press in 2011 (US), was shortlisted for both the T.S. Eliot Prize and Wales Book of the Year. *The Zoo Father* (Seren, 2001) and *The Huntress* (Seren, 2005) were also shortlisted for the T.S. Eliot Prize, and *The Zoo Father* was a Poetry Book Society Recommend-ation. Her debut collection, *Heart of a Deer*, was published by Enitharmon in 1998.

In 2004 the Poetry Book Society selected her for Next Generation Poets and *Mslexia* magazine named her one of the ten best new women poets of the decade.

She was Poetry Editor of *Poetry London* from 1989 to 2005, is a co-founding tutor of The Poetry School and co-edited

Tying the Song (Enitharmon, 2000), the first anthology from The Poetry School. She teaches poetry courses in the galleries at Tate Modern, tutors for the Arvon Foundation, Taliesin Trust and the Poetry School, and was Royal Literary Fund Fellow at the Courtauld Institute of Art in 2011-12. She spent the first part of her life as a sculptor and trained at the Royal College of Art.

ACKNOWLEDGEMENTS

With grateful thanks to Arts Council England for their generous funding and their extraordinary belief in the Complete Works and everything it stands for. When funding bodies act with vision and commitment, anything is possible.

Thanks also to Bernardine Evaristo, MBE. Without her there would be no Complete Works. I am grateful to have the opportunity to take care of her brainchild for this stretch of the journey.

Thanks also to our UK Patron, Carol Ann Duffy, and the US patron, Kwame Dawes.

And thanks to the fantastic steering group: Malika Booker, Roger Robinson, Karen McCarthy Woolf, Michael Schmidt, Daljit Nagra, Bernardine Evaristo, Fiona Sampson, Jacob Sam-La Rose, Mel Larsen and Sue Lawther who schlepped over to my house for meetings, food and laughter and gave invaluable advice.

Thanks to all the wonderful poets and mentors for putting up with my eccentricities – that one goes out to the poets in particular – namely my insistence on continually reminding them that Western thought is not the only way and for finding any excuse to discuss Latin American influences.

A big thanks also to Spread the Word for their continued support and to Candida Ronald.

And finally, thanks to all those who read this anthology and to the extended family of The Complete Works II: all those artists who write outside of the mainstream and follow their own path.

Gracias.

Nathalie Teitler, Director, The Complete Works II

PREVIOUS PUBLICATIONS

Mona Arshi: 'Ghazal', *Poetry Review*, 102: 3 (Autumn 2013). 'Daughters', *The Rialto*, 80 (Spring/Summer 2014).

Jay Bernard: none of the poems included here has been previously published.

Kayo Chingonyi: 'The N Word (II)', 'The Cricket Test' and 'The Room' were published in *Poetry Review*.

Rishi Dastidar: '22 March, Working in an Office on Berners Street' was a finalist in the Cardiff International Poetry Competition and is published on their website.

Edward Doegar: 'Half-Ghazal' was published in *Poetry Review* 102: 4 (Winter 2012).

Inua Ellams: none of the poems included here has been previously published.

Sarah Howe: 'Tame', *Transom*, transomjournal.com, Issue 5.

Adam Lowe: 'The Kiss', 'Vada That', 'Tough Look', *Vada Magazine*, www.vadamagazine.com. 'Tryst with the Devil', *Flicker & Spark: A Contemporary Queer Anthology of Spoken Word and Poetry* (Lowbrow Press, 2013).

Eileen Pun: 'Some Common Whitethroat Chit-Chat' and 'Lesser Whitethroat', *Birdbook III* (Sidekick Books, 2014); 'Studio Apartment: Sunday', *Clinic III*, 2013.

Warsan Shire: 'The Ugly Daughter', 'Haram', *teaching my mother how to give birth* (flipped eye, 2011).

Photographers: Aaron Corkin (Adam Lowe), Renée Doegar (Edward Doegar), Alice O'Brien (Jay Bernard), Amanda Pepper Photography (Mona Arshi), Kam Phung (Eileen Pun), Julia Ward (Inua Ellams), Naomi Woddis (Rishi Dastidar, Karen McCarthy Woolf).